14 Steps to Awaken the
SACRED FEMININE

"The faster we awaken the Sacred Feminine within all of us, the faster we can save the world. Don't delay. Drink in the wisdom of Norton and Starbird, who offer Mary Magdalene as the archetype of the Divine Bride of love, sensuality, and wholeness."

KAREN TATE, AUTHOR OF *SACRED PLACES OF GODDESS: 108 DESTINATIONS* AND *WALKING AN ANCIENT PATH: REBIRTHING GODDESS ON PLANET EARTH*

"Joan Norton and Margaret Starbird's suggestions for approaching the encounter with Mary Magdalene integrate some of the most precious traditions known to women's history: building caring communities, gathering together as a way of birthing new life and knowledge, and sharing devotional experience."

MARTHA MATHEWS LIBSTER, PH.D., R.N., HISTORIAN AND AUTHOR OF *ENLIGHTENED CHARITY* AND *HERBAL DIPLOMATS*

"As a sexual abuse survivor, this is a book I celebrate! Sexual abuse thrives in cultures like ours that banish the Sacred Feminine, and here is a book that shows how to awaken her and bring her back. The very thought is healing."

SANDRA POPE, AUTHOR OF *GROWING UP WITHOUT THE GODDESS: A JOURNEY THROUGH SEXUAL ABUSE TO THE SACRED EMBRACE OF MARY MAGDALENE*

"Joan Norton and Margaret Starbird have created a link to the long-hidden mystery of the holy marriage and family of Jesus and Mary Magdalene. This loving journey is shared in simple and graceful ways, allowing us to discover the Feminine Face of God, follow the signs, and practice in community and as individuals. I highly recommend beginning your own journey."

TINA CAREY, AUTHOR OF *GOD'S MESSENGERS FOR TODAY'S WOMEN*

"*14 Steps to Awaken the Sacred Feminine* embodies the leadership spirit of the Magdalene and invites us into her mysteries through personal experiences, thoughtful scholarship, and guided meditations. Norton and Starbird have written a book that shows Mary Magdalene is both an ancient representation of the sacred feminine and a potent role model for contemporary women."

KRIS OSTER, PH.D., COFOUNDER OF GAIA FESTIVAL

"Joan and Margaret deliver the story of Mary Magdalene in a way that puts into balance the truth of the Sacred Feminine. I feel within my very DNA that the oppression and suffering of the feminine that has occurred through all time has somehow been put right. I have been inspired to begin a Magdalene Circle in my own community, and I know women everywhere will be feeling the same call after reading this very important material."

CARRIE WOODBURN, INTEGRATIVE ENERGY HEALER

14 Steps to Awaken the
SACRED FEMININE

WOMEN IN THE CIRCLE
OF MARY MAGDALENE

JOAN NORTON AND
MARGARET STARBIRD

ILLUSTRATED BY ALEXIS HARTMAN

Bear & Company
Rochester, Vermont

Bear & Company
One Park Street
Rochester, Vermont 05767
www.BearandCompanyBooks.com

Bear & Company is a division of Inner Traditions International

Library of Congress Cataloging-in-Publication Data

Norton, Joan.
  14 steps to awaken the sacred feminine : women in the circle of Mary Magdalene
/ Joan Norton and Margaret Starbird ; illustrated by Alexis Hartman.
      p. cm.
  ISBN 978-1-59143-091-9 (pbk.)
  1. Mary Magdalene, Saint—Meditations. 2. Christian women—Prayers and
devotions. I. Starbird, Margaret, 1942– II. Title. III. Title: Fourteen steps to
awaken the sacred feminine.
  BS2485.N67 2009
  226'.092—dc22

                                                                    2008051219

Printed and bound in the United States by P. A. Hutchison

10 9 8 7 6 5 4 3 2 1

Text design and layout by Priscilla Baker
This book was typeset in Garamond Premier Pro with Shelley and Gill Sans used
as display typefaces

To contact the authors visit their websites. Joan Norton can be reached through
www.MaryMagdaleneWithin.com, and Margaret Starbird can be reached through
www.MargaretStarbird.net.

Thank you to all the women who have been
a part of "Our Lady, Queen of the Angels,"
the Los Angeles Magdalene Circle.
I am so grateful to you for helping
to bring Her home.

Contents

PART ONE

The Lessons of the Magdalene

PART TWO

*Prayers and Poems to Complement
the Lessons*

A Note of Deep Gratitude to Margaret Starbird

I've heard this said by woman after woman, "And then I read *The Woman with the Alabaster Jar* and everything changed, my mind lit up with hunger for more information. It put me on an entirely different spiritual path and I realized what I'd been searching for. She gave me new hope." Comments like this go on and on in appreciation for Margaret's first book.

Margaret has said that she was led to her theological insights on the Sacred Complement paradigm in Christianity by intuitive perceptions and prophetic messages given to her and her friends in their prayer group in the 1970s and '80s. Research followed intuitive perception, which for me is another validation of the return of the Sacred Feminine dimension of feeling and intuition. When the Bride was denied by Christianity, the spirituality centered in the body with its feelings and intuitions was thrown away, so of course that's the dimension through which She is returning.

Margaret's own personal story of the crisis her revelations created for her, and the dark night of the soul that ensued, is well told in *The Goddess in the Gospels,* which I hope you will read. She went on to illuminate the truth of the presence of the Bride, the Sacred Complement to Jesus, in piece after piece of scripture, and to illuminate the archetypal underpinnings of the sacred marriage at the core of Christianity.

She is at the heart of this book and of the idea to create Magdalene Circles. Nothing can substitute for reading her books; I encourage each group to read and talk about them. There are many beautiful images of the old paintings of Mary Magdalene in Margaret's books as well, which are also a stimulus for interesting discussions. Once our eyes are opened to the common symbols used to portray Mary Magdalene, we tend to see her everywhere, and rightly so. She is at the very center.

Thank you, Margaret, for sharing so much with so many.

An Hour or Two in the Life of Our Magdalene Circle

We are gathered today to be with Mary Magdalene. The chairs are placed in a circle in the back room of the Woman's Club of Hollywood, a venerable old wooden-frame building with lots of history of women bettering their lives. In the center of the circle on the floor I've put a colorful cotton cloth of earthy fall colors, about half a square yard, just enough to create a sacred space. On the cloth I've also put water in a pretty bowl, the Living Water of the Divine Feminine who comes to us as Mary Magdalene. I have placed a green crystal rock that holds a little candle, along with a few other rocks from my garden. A small vase of flowers is there too, flowers that are fall blooming. For this meeting I have brought in a bit of my garden compost, telling the group that we are reaping the composted reward of Mary Magdalene being thrown out with the trash those two thousand years ago. Mary had been assigned to the garbage heap but now she's turned to gold.

We start by lighting a candle and saying a prayer or two or three in recognition and honoring of Mary Magdalene and of ourselves. We are beginning our Magdalene Circle again for the year, so I say something about our heritage of women in circles, circles with the power to change the lives of the women in them and therefore the world. Jean Shinoda Bolen's *The Millionth Circle* has reminded me that we got the vote because women in Seneca Falls met in someone's kitchen and decided it needed to be so. We circled in the 1960s and '70s to start trends toward equal pay and shared family responsibilities. Through time and history we women have circled with our friends to help each other go through difficult times, and sometimes we have finished a quilt together, working together as a community.

Apparently practitioners of the original religions used to circle in great large numbers. Stonehenge and many sacred hill formations remind us of the strength of consciousness of the circle. And now the crop circles have come to those same Celtic lands that hold many early blueprints of Christianity, intensifying the mysteries of Earth's intelligence beyond our comprehension. She is creating circles with mathematical relationships that convey ageless wisdom, through the physics that is one of God's foundational languages.

So here we are, women in a circle around a sacred altar, devotional to Mary the Holy Magdalene. In a newly started circle everyone needs to know each other so that we can trust and feel safe in sharing spiritual experiences together. Have you ever been in a classroom under fluorescent lights and been asked to reveal your thoughts to people you didn't really know? That's just what doesn't work for spirituality or anything else personal. To begin to get to know each other, we tell our names and answer the questions I have posed: "What has been your experience with religion? What has made Mary Magdalene interesting to you?" This can be the basis for a whole meeting, as you can well imagine.

We like to begin each circle with music. Today in the background we played a recording by Mary Black, the wonderful Irish singer, until we did the spoken meditation. We also bring food to share and we may eat whenever we feel like it. Why wait when there's a table full of good food sitting there?

Today I have decided to share a scriptural reading: John 12:1–3, "The Anointing at Bethany." I believe that this is the wedding scene of our Christian story, when Mary Magdalene chooses Jesus as her sacred Bridegroom. The archetype of union is the most central organizing pattern of the mind and heart of God: from the union of opposites—male energies and female energies—comes the subsequent birth of new possibilities. It is the mystery from which all life, all that is created in the physical world, flows, and it is certainly our inner psychological story. The theme of attraction, marriage, and children—life, growth, and inner development—is repeated over and over in all its incredible variations in our dreams and in art.

It was this central mystery that Jesus and Mary Magdalene consciously enacted at her home in Bethany, on the Mount of Olives, as it was prefigured in ancient rites of "sacred marriage" indigenous to the Middle East. Margaret Starbird has said that she thinks Jesus had the conscious intention to restore the Divine Feminine in creating this sacred marriage scene with Mary Magdalene. Together they represent Wholeness. We certainly can expect our God to honor the very life She/He created by giving us a creation story that makes sense in the life we live. A celibate God never made sense and has certainly caused terrible distortions in religious life.

We talk about these things in our circle and everyone has thoughts and feelings and experiences to tell. I often remind our group that sharing isn't required and that we honor and value silence as a contribution as well. Sometimes I say that forced expression can be very difficult for sensitive women. I myself have been very shy and have felt grateful for elder women who understood my quietness. Many women feel like sharing after a few meetings, when they have had the opportunity to see that the group is safe and not competitive.

A particular kind of sharing that we often include is our dreams. Magdalene Circles are likely to stimulate dreams because our souls are interested in our spiritual development and the circles encourage that. Dream guidance is simply incredible, deeply and intricately personal. I've been a student of my own dream life for forty years and I've practiced Jungian psychotherapy for thirty. So I make dream sharing a part of everything I do with people and it's a part of our circle as well. I find that women have the most amazing wisdom to add when talking over a symbolic dream image. And of course, there may be dreams of Mary Magdalene herself to treasure.

Many times the spiritual imagery and themes that come from one person's dream are useful for all the members of the group. One woman brought a dream to our group that was helpful to everyone. She dreamed she saw Queen Elizabeth II and the queen had handmaidens who spoke Gaelic. This led to a nice discussion about Celtic spirituality as a way of Christianity that was grounded in honoring the feminine spirit and the body. We began finding Celtic prayers to say.

We follow our discussion with a spoken meditation, often preceded by a prayer, to help set the tone. As today we are beginning another year's cycle of meetings, my meditation is "Remembering Ourselves in Her." Its purpose is to help us remember that we are not separate from God and that our bodies give us the gift of experiencing this connection to the Divine. I create the rhythm for going within by guiding the group to breathe deeply and slowly. After I've stopped reading the meditation I say, "Continue to sit quietly with your eyes closed for a time, then open them again when you feel ready." The atmosphere of the room shifts to a very peaceful, harmonious feeling. Then I ask if anyone wants to talk about her meditative experience.

Sometimes the experience is that of a very relaxing twenty minutes or so, simply a time to stop the feelings of go-go-go. And sometimes an inner image develops in one of the women's meditative time, an image of deep meaning. Women in our group have at times had inner "visitations" from the Magdalene herself. There is a body of literature about people who've had experiences of Jesus coming to them and helping them in the most uniquely personal ways, and now we are hearing more and more of this with Mary Magdalene. She's been waiting a long time.

One of our group members had the experience of Mary coming to her with a crosier and placing it firmly against her spine, while communicating that she should straighten up and get to work. When this woman shared her experience with the group, she recognized it as implying that she needed to pay more attention to her spiritual work and path. Another woman in our group felt the Beloved Mother as well as Mary Magdalene came to her in a meditation, offering advice about becoming a mother. The two Marys both said, "Why don't you come more frequently to us for help?"

The directness and clarity of such experiences is startling and the messages often answer questions that the person didn't quite know she was asking. Most of us have heard all our lives that "the Kingdom of God is within," but it's still a big surprise when a piece of wisdom advice so perfectly suited to our current struggles arises in meditation. We also know that "not a hair on your head goes uncounted." This means, of course, that our precise place on our life's path is observed and known and we can expect help for it. The Queendom of God is also within and comes to us with help.

While some women are experienced with visitations and familiar with symbolic guidance, others are not. Our way of sharing allows us to help one another in understanding the messages being given. And, regardless of the content of the meditation, all of us benefit from the peaceful, renewing quiet time.

After the meditation and sharing the circle feels complete for the day, so we close with a prayer. Then it is time for visiting, more eating, looking at books and art. We have a book table, a lending library of Magdalene books. I have placed Margaret Starbird's books there, of course, and also those of Jean-Yves LeLoup; circle members contribute other ones as well. All of our upcoming circles will be personalized by the inclusion of the books we each have read and liked. Sometimes a whole meeting can be spent sharing the insights we have gained and reactions we have to these books.

I also like to have as many pictures of Mary Magdalene with us as possible, both historical artwork and modern artwork. When we started our Los Angeles Magdalene Circle we discovered that quite a few of the women painted, so we began sharing artwork. No critiquing of course, just the artist talking about her own experience while doing the painting. It feels like the Sacred Feminine is working through the minds and hearts of women to create new symbols for our time.

I set the time for the circle to be about an hour and a half but it usually drifts toward two. We leave each other until the next Magdalene Circle, taking a little bit more of the Sacred Feminine into our daily lives.

One of the ways we encourage the presence of the Divine in our lives in between our meetings is by journaling. I was the facilitator for a couple of years for a program called Companions in Christ at my church of the time, Hollywood United Methodist. It's a good program that encourages the personal inner experience of Jesus's teachings. The program included weekly private journaling, which provided an opportunity to respond deeply to spiritual questions. Jesus said that God is inside us, indicating perhaps that the Christian way was meant to be a path to personal enlightenment, always an inner process. When the Church left out Mary Magdalene, it also attempted to throw out the teachings of the inner path to enlightenment experience. But throughout history there have always been those who have known that the inner path must be trod to know God, and journaling nurtures that process. I know so many wonderfully deep intuitive women who have so much to offer from their inner worlds, whose riches are revealed through writing, or through drawing, another of God's primary languages.

USING THIS BOOK TO GUIDE YOUR OWN MAGDALENE CIRCLE

The fourteen lessons provided in this book are offered to you as a guide to support the awakening of the Sacred Feminine in your circle. Naturally, your group may evolve a different "course of study," but these lessons offer a good framework of essential aspects of Mary Magdalene and what she offers to us all. The lessons we offer are an outline that you can build upon and change to suit the needs and interests of your unique group and how you wish to create its spiritual center.

Opening Prayer. It is nice to begin with lighting a candle and then sharing a prayer. Part 2 of this book provides a selection of poems and prayers for your use. The prayers and poems were gathered, and in some cases written, by Susan Kehoe-Jergens, of our Los Angeles Magdalene Circle, and include a Magdalene Rosary developed by Margaret Starbird. We often begin our time of spoken meditation with a prayer or a poem as well, to help focus our attention.

Reading. The prayer can be followed by a reading related to the chosen topic, such as the illuminating theological essays of Margaret Starbird that are included here. In your circle you may want to add other readings as well.

Reflections and Sharing. The purpose of a Magdalene Circle is for the participants both to learn about Mary Magdalene and to talk about themselves. A Magdalene Circle is not a church model of worship, but rather a way to feel the presence of the sacred within. To foster this, I have provided a section for each lesson that includes my own reflections, along with suggestions and questions to deepen and personalize your own experience of the Sacred Feminine. It can be read out loud to initiate an unstructured time of open sharing, time for talking over the subject and relating it to your personal life experiences.

Spoken Meditation. In order to connect our personal lives and
spiritual journeys to Mary Magdalene's stories, I've written a
short meditation to be spoken for each subject. Of course, you
might decide to change and adapt the meditations, adding your
own flavor. Whether you use these meditations or some others,
keep in mind that breathing works better than anything to help
us go inward to where Divinity lives. Just breathe. And . . . read . . .
slowly. The words create a pathway inward and the silent space
at the end of the meditation allows each person's own soul to
give her an image or an insight, or to have a deeply restful few
minutes. After concluding the meditation you can again gently
invite sharing.

Closing Prayer. The circle can be closed with a poem or prayer, perhaps one selected from the collection provided by Susan Kehoe-
Jergens in part 2, or one chosen by your group. As Susan notes,
closing with a prayer provides emotional closure as well as continuity to the next meeting. Your group might also decide to recite
the Magdalene Rosary together to open or close the meeting.

Journal Questions. I have also included journaling questions for
each lesson in case your circle wants more personal spiritual experience than the meetings can hold. In fact, a circle's whole intention can be formed around journaling and sharing your insights.

Do you feel ready to find a few interested friends and start a
Magdalene Circle? I hope so! We are all reclaiming what is ours.

Some Practical Thoughts

I have often thought of quilting bees while writing this book. How
many women will fit comfortably around a quilting frame? The old
photographs show between four and nine women sitting together, nee-
dles poised, looking seriously at the camera. That's a good number for
a Magdalene Circle as well. Then, if your group runs for an hour and

a half or two, there will be enough time for everyone to have a chance to talk.

Keep the group as steady in members as you can, because trust will build between you and you won't have to start your stories all over again when someone new joins. Also, joining an established group can be difficult for a new person to handle. I should mention confidentiality here. It goes without saying that you should make a conscious and stated agreement with each other in the beginning to not tell each other's stories outside the group. It is destructive and will cause your group to quickly dissolve.

Where will you meet? The same place or trade off to different houses? There's an advantage to being in the same place each time because the room itself becomes a source of comfort and familiar privacy. How often will you meet? Naturally, the more frequently you meet, the more support you will give to each other's lives.

You may know loving men who are also interested in knowing more about Mary Magdalene and the Sacred Union, and that will be another question to ask yourselves. How do we feel about opening our group to men? Opinions will vary, depending on your friends' experiences with men in their lives. There have been quite a few men interested in joining our Los Angeles group, but we have kept it as a women's group. It is the softer side of men's hearts that is touched by Mary Magdalene and I feel hopeful that many are interested in knowing more and will want to be included in our circles.

You might consider taking turns doing the readings of Margaret's essays and my reflections and spoken meditations, as well as the opening and closing prayers. Women are often shy about this, but as you get to know each other you'll feel more confident about being in the reader's role. It feels good to say spiritual words, which is something that has been traditionally denied women in many, many churches. Women have told me that when they've read out loud the words of Sacred Feminine spirituality, they have felt like the Inquisition was waiting at the door to take them away. That's how deep the denial of the Bride is. But in the safety of an encouraging Magdalene Circle, these old fears can be replaced by confidence and inspiration.

As you create your Magdalene Circle, you may want to discuss whether or not to share your dreams, because they reveal so much personal information. They can bring forth images of the raw pain of all the ways women have been abused physically and violated spiritually. Many times the dreamer herself doesn't realize what she is revealing. We all probably intuitively recognize when another woman is in deep emotional trouble, and certainly a dream can show this. Sometimes the emotional difficulty is too much for a circle of women friends to handle. Then the group may have to demonstrate compassionate toughness and tell a member that she might need individual help from a therapist. That said, dreams can certainly bring incredible imagery and insight into the spiritual subjects that such a circle will explore.

A good way to deal with dreams in a group is to have the attitude of simple receptivity and honoring rather than any kind of analysis. Another helpful approach is the Jungian way of amplification, adding what you know from mythology, religion, and everyday knowledge to the dream's images. This places your own personal stories in the context of universal themes.

Altars

I hope you will want to create altars for each meeting as a centering focus and a visual inspiration. They can be very simple; a single candle will do the job. But it's fun and spiritually satisfying to create an altar, and fun to take turns doing it. Each woman will have her own style. Since I love cloth I always start there, choosing a well-worn soft linen tea cloth or a piece of fabric with seasonal colors. I usually have a few simple flowers on my altars because their presence honors Mother Earth's beauty and harmony. If I know we're going to be talking about a particular Mary Magdalene story, such as "Journey in the Boat with No

Oars," I find something reminiscent of a boat. I have a crescent-shaped basket that my mother Betty made, which I often use to represent the boat. Her beautiful basket seems to work for a few other themes as well: set on its side it becomes the cave tomb for the "Descent to the Tomb" story.

The important thing is to be intuitive about the altar, to walk around your own house choosing what appeals to you from your own life. I'm always surprised that I have the necessary symbols for the Magdalene stories "hidden in plain sight" in the everyday objects of my home. But that's what we are realizing about her, isn't it? God's primary language isn't words; it's images. It is images that stay with us and influence us. That is why we create an altar devotional to Mary Magdalene and that's why we put it in the center of our circle.

USING THIS BOOK FOR YOUR INDIVIDUAL SPIRITUAL JOURNEYING

Not every woman has access to friends who want to start a Magdalene Circle, and some of us just want to practice our spiritual life in private. I am, "by design," an introverted person and my spiritual learning path has been very private, so I understand and honor this way. Even though Mary Magdalene was the original Sacred Partner, she's often not accepted that way now, and not all women feel safe to express themselves spiritually in nontraditional ways. Whatever the reason, some of us simply want to be alone with our own thoughts and feelings in our spiritual journeying.

To use this book on your own, you can read Margaret's essay, followed by my reflections and meditation, then choose a quiet time and place for peaceful contemplation of them. As Margaret has suggested in *The Feminine Face of Christianity,* there are many ways to "set the stage" for a spiritual experience, ways to encourage a receptive state of mind and heart. More and more women I know have created a private altar in their homes, somewhere to place their most meaningful statues, pictures, candles, and flowers—a place to come for spiritual focus. Another method for going within that is growing in popularity is the prayer-stole meditation. A prayer stole over your head and shoulders creates your own private sacred space. Margaret suggests that to get in touch with the loving energy of the Blessed Mother or Mary Magdalene, select or create a prayer stole, drape it over your head and shoulders, then sit very quietly, breathing peacefully, waiting expectantly for the "Lady" to be present to you.

You can use the journal questions as a way to deepen your self-questioning and contemplation and nourish your own personal and unique relationship with Mary Magdalene. The feminine spirit is so very receptive. Your soul is always seeking to listen to you and to answer you. You can naturally expect to be answered as you ask the questions of your own inner wisdom. And so, put on your lovely prayer shawl, and create a private space to read, write, and go within.

Even if you go through this book by yourself, you certainly will not be alone on the spiritual plane. "When one or more is gathered in my name, I will be there" applies to both the feminine and the masculine presence of God. Whether we are sitting alone or in a circle, we are the feet and hands of the indwelling Divine, and Mary Magdalene will guide us to our own sacred Wholeness.

PART ONE

The Lessons of the Magdalene

It Was Foretold

MARGARET STARBIRD

Reclaiming the Bride and Beloved

All four of the canonical Christian Gospels agree—a woman came to Jesus while he was reclining at a banquet and anointed him with precious unguent of nard from the alabaster jar she was carrying. In the three earliest Gospels, the woman is not named, but John's Gospel names her. In case we overlook the first mention, he names her twice. She is Mary, the sister of Lazarus. And in this Gospel, when Judas complains about the wasted value of her perfume, Jesus says, "Let her keep it for the day of my burial." Several chapters later, it is Mary Magdalene who comes before dawn to mourn at the tomb of her Beloved and—in all four Gospels and throughout millennia of Christian art—it is this Mary, the one called "the Magdalene," who carries the alabaster jar.

What is the meaning of this image of the holy woman carrying her precious container, desolate and bereft, approaching the tomb of her tortured and mutilated Bridegroom King? Who is she but the Daughter of Zion, ultimate representative of her nation, and the personification of her land and people as Bride of God?

In Neolithic times (7000–3500 BCE) a royal bride chose her bridegroom from among the available men and was united with him in the rites of *hieros gamos* ("holy wedding"). The princess represented her land and people, and the anointing of the king was her royal prerogative. The "anointed one" was king by virtue of marriage to her. The couple consummated their union in the bridal chamber, and the joy and blessing flowed from their union out into the crops and herds and to the people of their domain. These ancestors celebrated the Life Force—the sacred union and harmony of opposite energies and the cosmic balance manifest in all creation. Numerous god and goddess couples of ancient pagan peoples celebrated similar rites of sacred marriage, acknowledging and honoring the cosmic dance of masculine and feminine energies and the eternal cycles manifested by the Life Force. Among these fertility deities of the ancient Middle East were Osiris and his sister-bride Isis, whose liturgical poetry, published as *The Burden of Isis,* by J. T. Dennis (Forgotten Books, 1918), was the source of the erotic, ecstatic Song of Solomon found in the Hebrew Bible. In this beautiful poem, the bride is separated from her beloved and then reunited with him again, one of the defining elements of the hieros gamos mythology, which includes the torture and death of the bridegroom king and his resurrection in the garden on the third day after his death.

In the Song of Solomon, the bride is black, swarthy from her labor in her brothers' vineyards. The fragrance of her nard wafts around her bridegroom as he is reclining at a banquet. Later, as she wanders through the streets in search of her bridegroom, the guardians of the walls come upon her. They beat her and wound her and strip her mantle from her. She is left disconsolate. She is the desecrated bride, the denigrated feminine, defamed and disowned: the abandoned one, prostrate on the ground.

But in the closing lines of the Song, their separation is ended. The beloveds are reconciled and reunited. They celebrate their love in the orchard of pomegranates. It is this same "never-ending story" of the eternal return of love and life that is at the heart of the Christian Gospels. It is time to reclaim our heritage—the sacred reunion of the archetypal Bride and Bridegroom at the heart of the Christian mythology.

REFLECTIONS and SHARING

We're here today to call upon the Queen of Heaven, the Sacred Feminine energy of God, and to know it as ourselves. All philosophies, all religions, have representations of the Divine Queen, the "other half" of God, and ours in Western civilization is Mary Magdalene. In the Old Testament it was foretold that the Holy Bride and the divinity of the feminine spirit would be restored from its state of defilement; we believe that this restoration was meant to be through the sacred marriage of Jesus and Mary the Magdalene at her Bethany home on the Mount of Olives.

Many are researching and discussing the emergence of Mary Magdalene, the reexamination of her place in the Bible, and her place in the history of Christianity. In this Magdalene Circle we are following the research of Margaret Starbird, who has inspired so many to reconsider the Bride. You may know of other researchers and want to share what you've read. Christianity belongs to us and Mary Magdalene belongs to us and we want to include her in the story again.

I'm grateful for the stories of Mary Magdalene because she fully lived a woman's life of love and relationship, while also being a source of special spiritual knowledge. In her we find guidance for both the inner life of the spirit and the outer life of love. That has always been the role of the feminine face of God. I'm grateful for the pathways to self-knowledge that Mary Magdalene's stories provide, and it's her stories that will be the basis of our Magdalene Circle's work together.

Forever we have been told to seek the Kingdom within. Now at the beginning of a new millennium and a new era, we seek to understand the feminine energy of God, which we can call the "Queendom within." Together they are a whole known as the Divine.

Let's get started knowing each other. We'll take time now to say our names, to share where we've come from spiritually, and to say what our curiosities are about Mary Magdalene.

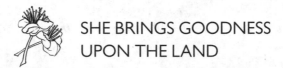

SHE BRINGS GOODNESS UPON THE LAND

Close your eyes and feel your feet on the floor. Breathe a simple breath . . . and another breath even slower than the first one . . . and now another breath . . . still so slowly.

You are safe here in this room, with your feet on the floor and the floor upon Mother Earth . . . your feet are feeling the warmth of the earth, so secure and so safe . . .

Breathe again deeply and slowly . . . your feet are heavy now and comfortable on the floor . . .

Once upon a time it was foretold that the Bridegroom would have a Bride and that goodness would be upon the land and healing would come from their union . . .

Breathe . . .

It was foretold that the two halves of God would be together as One . . .

Wholeness is our birthright . . . Breathe deeply and remember your whole and sacred self . . .

There was a time when we women knew ourselves to be in sacred partnership, knew ourselves to be the Sacred Complement to the Bridegroom . . . knew that masculine and feminine God meet within each human being . . .

Breathe again slowly . . .

Breathe into a place within your heart, a place of knowing yourself as Sacred Partner . . . as soul partner . . . as Bride and Beloved . . .

It was foretold . . . and let that time be now . . . and let that sacred vessel be me . . .

Sit in silence for a while and let images or feelings surface within you.

(Allow 5 or 10 minutes.)

Open your eyes and come back into the room, as you are ready.

What were your experiences during this meditation? Is there anything you would like to share with us all? And please remember that sharing isn't necessary; your presence here in meditation adds so much to our group.

XX   JOURNAL QUESTIONS

In the Song of Songs (5:7) the bride says, "They beat me and wounded me and stripped my mantle from me." In what ways do you feel women have been treated disrespectfully by your religion?

Describe your experience of a "dark night of the soul" in relation to your religious beliefs.

LESSON 2

I Thought She Was a Prostitute from Magdala

MARGARET STARBIRD
Called "the Magdalene"

In the Gospels of the Christian Scriptures Mary Magdalene is portrayed as one of the women who supported the entourage of Jesus and his ministry with her personal wealth. But more importantly, she is portrayed as the most loyal and most devoted of all the women who accompanied Jesus. Each of the authors of the four canonical Gospels places Mary Magdalene at the cross and at the tomb. In Matthew's Gospel we read, "Mary Magdalene and the other Mary went to the tomb." Clearly Mary Magdalene is the preeminent woman in the Gospel narratives.

One of the symbols often associated with Mary Magdalene is tears. She cries over the death of her brother Lazarus and Jesus is moved by her tears. She cries over the feet of Jesus at the banquet in Bethany and wipes her tears from his feet with her hair. She cries again at the tomb on Easter morning; she is distraught, having found the tomb empty, not knowing where they have taken the body of her beloved. "Woman, why are you crying?" Jesus asks her. The word used in the original Greek of the text is *gune,* which can mean either "wife" or "woman," depending on the context. This poignant scene is an echo of a very ancient prophecy from the book of Micah in the Hebrew Bible, a prophecy that was written in about 700 BCE. The prophecy is addressed to the "Magdal-eder," a personification of the Daughter of Sion.

> *As for you, O Magdal-eder,*
> *To you dominion shall be restored.*
> *Why are you crying aloud?*
> *Have you no king? Has your counselor*
>   *perished?*
> *To Babylon must you go*
> *And from there you shall be rescued.*
> *Nations shall gather against you; they will call*
>   *you unclean.*
>
>   MICAH 4:8–11

The Aramaic word *magdala* can refer to a tower, citadel, or fortress, so the literal translation of Magdal-eder is "watchtower of the flock." She is crying over her deceased king and teacher and is then sent into foreign exile, defiled and defamed. But according to this prophecy, she shall someday be rescued from her exile. Could it be that the early Christians who wrote the Gospels recognized the beloved wife of Jesus in this passage that seems to sum up her story in a nutshell? The Aramaic title *Magdala* (Tower) connotes strength and power. This woman who mourns at the tomb of the deceased king is the representative of her land and people. She is the royal bride whose prerogative it was in ancient times to anoint the king and to cry at his tomb.

For centuries Mary Magdalene's power and voice were stolen when she was called "prostitute" and "penitent"—words insinuating that she had led a dissolute and sinful life. In 1969 the Roman Catholic Church admitted that there was no scriptural justification whatsoever for these scurrilous epithets. In fact, Mary was given the epithet "the Magdalene" as an honorary title signaling her status as First Lady, Bride, and Beloved. In calling her name, invoking her return, we end her long silence in exile. Behold, she stands at the threshold of our consciousness, awaiting our invitation.

REFLECTIONS and SHARING

Did you know that there were four towns named Magdala during the time of our early Christian story? And that the one now mistakenly identified by tour guides as Mary Magdalene's hometown was in those days called by an entirely different Greek name, Taricheae? No one would have called her "Mary of Magdala" because her home didn't have that name during her time, nor were women in the Gospels identified by place names. There is no proof at all that the word *Magdalene* was derived from a town called Magdala. Magdalene is more likely her title, a title of honor indicating her royal stature, her place as "Watchtower" or "Stronghold of the Flock" and Sacred Partner to Jesus, the "Good Shepherd."

Reaching back through to early times for facts about Mary Magdalene is reaching back into times of dark consciousness for women, a time when wives were commonly not even named in documents. No wonder researchers make errors and assumptions about Mary Magdalene. But some things can't lie. Of the eight lists of women in the New Testament, Mary Magdalene comes first in all but one. It's as if she is the First Lady.

There was no Mary of Magdala but there was a woman whom people seemed to recognize as the Bride prophesized by the Old Testament, who was honored in the very popular Song of Songs. People of those times knew that a messiah wouldn't come without a "co-messiah" wife. She was the one who would return from exile and cause the land and life to be fertile again. She was the deeply honored Divine Feminine embodied in a woman living an earthly life. People recognized her as "the Magnificent" and "the Great," both titles that had always belonged to the feminine half of God. Certainly the root word of the title *Magdalene* comes from *mag,* an ancient word for Mother God. She is the only person in the New Testament besides Jesus to have a title of such stature.

When stories circulated about the anointing of Jesus, the sacred marriage on the Mount of Olives, it was most likely recognized that the Bride had returned to claim her Sacred Masculine partner, Jesus.

We all know by now that the label of "prostitute" was falsely placed on Mary Magdalene by the church fathers in their efforts to consolidate their power and their story during the first few hundred years of Christianity. Even the modern church has officially corrected the prostitute story, but it has not put any effort into restoring her stature. That has been left to the women of today who intuitively recognize the presence of the Sacred Feminine, come to heal the wasteland.

Now we have the eyes to see that Jesus was not alone, was not a celibate lone male god. He was in sacred partnership with a soul of magnificence and he was in physical partnership with a woman of great heart, Mary called the Magdalene.

Where do your thoughts and ideas go as we talk about Mary Magdalene in this new way?

THE BRIDE IN DARKNESS AND HIDING

Breathe . . . breathe again slowly . . . feel the steadiness of your feet upon the floor. There is warmth there, as though your feet are touching sun-warmed sand or earth . . . feel your feet completely . . . their strength is everything to you.

Breathe again deeply and slowly . . .

The warm energy of your body meets the warming energy of the earth through your feet. The earth and your body love and appreciate each other . . . earth to body goes the flow.

Breathe slowly as quietness comes to you in this safe and secure place . . .

Now remember that there has been a part of you that had to go into darkness and hiding through so much history and so much personal life . . .

Breathe . . . remember that Mary Magdalene was thrown out of her own story, stripped of her mantle . . .

Feel the ways in which you too have been in hiding . . .

But exile is over now . . . the Magdalene returns within women everywhere.

She is no longer forlorn or gaunt . . .

Breathe deeply again . . .

She has chosen this time to return to her sacred role . . .

Breathe deeply as you let that dark time go . . .

Slowly breathe as she says to you, "Let's not hide . . . I am with you now."

Take some time in silence to feel the Magdalene's way of being with you . . . in this time. . . in your life.

(A silent several minutes.)

And when you feel ready, open your eyes and come back into the room.

———

Would you like to share any of your meditation experiences?

XX JOURNAL QUESTIONS

When you were young, what images of God did you have?

What difference do you think it would have made if you had heard stories of an equally important Divine Woman?

What spiritual stories of a "special woman" were you given?

Other Ways We Know She Is the Bride

MARGARET STARBIRD

Symbolic Value of "H Magdalhnh"

The identity of the Mary called "the Magdalene" is powerfully reinforced by the symbolic value of her Greek title, H Magdalhnh. Based on the ancient practice of sacred geometry and the calculation of a canon of sacred numbers by Greek mathematicians and philosophers, certain numbers held significant symbolic meaning. Gematria—a literary device by which these symbolic or sacred numbers were encoded in the phrases of written texts—permeates both Testaments of the Judeo-Christian scriptures. Not surprisingly, one of the most significant phrases that express a symbolic number is Mary's title, H Magdalhnh. Since both Hebrew and Greek alphabets assign a numeric value to each letter, the sum of all the letters in a given phrase can be easily added to determine its gematria. The sum of the letters of H Magdalhnh is 153, the number of the fishes in the net in the Gospel of John (20), a metaphor for the church of Christian converts, the "little fishes." Because Mary Magdalene represents the community or church (*ekklesia*) as the Bride of Christ, this passage helps us understand her true identity.

But behind the scenes, there is an even more powerful symbolic meaning of the 153 of H Magdalhnh. Among Greek geometers 153 was an abbreviation or "shorthand" reference to the square root of three, expressed as the ratio 265/153. In stating "153," the geometer was also denoting the shape called *Vesica Piscis* (Vessel of the Fish), which has been universally associated with the goddess of love and fertility, the "yoni," the "doorway to life," and "the womb." This shape, (), was known to the Greeks as the matrix or "mother" of all other forms and shapes. It is the shared space when two circles intersect through one another's centers and is associated with the idea of "Source" or "Sacred Cauldron." How entirely appropriate that the authors of the New Testament coined a title for Mary Magdalene that expressed this symbolic value of the Sacred Container identified with the Bride as representative of her land and people. It is significant that over two millennia of Christian art, this woman carries a sacred container in her hands, her alabaster jar of precious ointment used to anoint her Bridegroom King.

The name *Ihsous* (Jesus) has a sum by gematria of 888, while *Kyrios* (Lord) adds up to 800. When we multiply the 153 of Magdalene's title by 8, the product is 1224, which is the numeric value of *ichthyes*, "fishes." In light of the New Age dawning at the turn of the first century, it is highly significant that these numbers reflect the Lord and Lady of the Age of Pisces—the Age of the Fishes. The architects of the New Covenant were deliberately "coining" the names and titles of the "avatars" of the promised "age to come" whose zodiac symbol is so similar to the yin and yang symbol of the Orient. The numbers reflect the "sacred partnership" of the Fishes.

In early November 2005 the mosaic floor of a third-century prayer hall—the earliest ever discovered in Israel—was excavated in Megiddo, Israel. Imagine the surprise of those who examined the mosaic floor, donated by a Roman centurion "in honor of the god Jesus Christ," to discover the central mandala depicting two fishes, the zodiac symbol for Pisces. Before they honored the cross, the early Christians honored the Fishes. As the gematria of her title most clearly associates Mary Magdalene with both the symbolism of the Fishes and the Sacred Container—the Divine Feminine—she is the preeminent "Goddess in the Gospels."

REFLECTIONS and SHARING

One reason we've loved Mary Magdalene is because we were told how much Jesus loved her, even if we were told the wrong reasons. Our secret longing is to be as well loved as she was, by God and man. How confusing it has been to be told that she is such a sinner! It might almost make us want to go that way ourselves, just to get Jesus's love. Luckily, the real story is easier. It's the story of the naturalness and sacredness of love and union on all levels of being: body, mind, and soul. The natural story is of a Bridegroom and his own dearly Beloved, his Bride. This story of Sacred Complements is a pattern of God that is found in all the major religions. It's the most natural pattern of life all around us. Jesus and Mary Magdalene reflect it to us in our Christian story. It's the story of sacred union in all dimensions of life: the physical, the emotional, and the spiritual. As above, so below. As with God, so with us.

Maybe the early church fathers knew this despite themselves when they chose wedding poetry to be read on Mary Magdalene's Feast Day of July 22. Even while denying the Bride, they needed to have Mary Magdalene's loving nature expressed in the deepest of ways, in the rich poetry of wedding love. And maybe the fact that she is pictured as a royal bride in royal bride's clothing in painting after painting in century after century gives the deeper truth as well, the truth that could never really be hidden.

"All glorious is the king's daughter as she enters, her raiment threaded with gold; in embroidered apparel she is led to the king" (Psalm 45:14–15, "Nuptial Ode of the Messianic King").

In the ancient religions the word *anointing* was used to describe the royal bride's choosing of a bridegroom. It signified her formal acceptance of him into her bed and therefore as a protector of her land and her people. Only with the queen's acceptance could a king rule. In some dictionaries *anointed* and *messiah* are interchangeable words. "To anoint" is to choose a king, to give a king the blessing of the Sacred Feminine. Understanding this context begins to put Mary Magdalene in a different role and a different light, the light with which she was viewed by people of the time who gave to her a title fit for her role as "anointer" of her Bridegroom King.

As Margaret points out, during those early times of very little writing, words in Greek had number equivalents, which intensified their meaning. Spellings and titles were carefully crafted to underscore religious meanings and to elevate the spiritual associations to the word. The number equivalency of Mary Magdalene's title (153) identified her as the feminine half of God. She was given that title purposefully to indicate her status as Queen and Bride in the sacred marriage. She is that part of God that is the land, the life, the people. She represents life itself.

She's dressed as the Bride in gold embroidery and she carries a vessel of blessing. She loves and honors Jesus as the chosen Messiah, able to lead because of her blessing. Together they are "the Way."

Shall we share our reactions to these new ideas about the nature of anointing and Mary Magdalene's role?

REMEMBERING OURSELVES IN HER

Close your eyes and breathe very slowly and naturally . . .

Feel yourself on your chair and your chair on the floor and the floor on the earth . . . your body is relaxing completely . . .

Mary Magdalene is our Beloved Queen, our Bride of God . . . through her stories we know ourselves to be women of the Holy Feminine . . .

Breathe . . . no need to strain your mind elsewhere or to another time . . .

Simply be . . . here . . . now . . . breathe comfortably and slowly . . .

Remember that once upon a time there was a woman . . . like you . . .

In her mind she was intelligent . . . like you.

In her body she was a woman like yourself who felt the things you feel . . . all the ways you feel as a woman . . .

Breathe the remembrance of the deeper feelings that you've known in your bodylife . . .

The feelings that have brought you wisdom . . .

Mary Magdalene didn't separate herself from ordinary women's life . . .

Because of this we trust her . . .

Breathe . . . and breathe again . . .

Mary Magdalene is the "Way of the Heart," the heart divine that includes our feeling and our intuition . . .

She loved . . . Joy is also her name . . . breathe deeply into her joy . . .

Remember your own heart, with the wisdom of its intuition and its feelings . . . your heart is connected to her heart . . . to the heart of Mary Magdalene . . .

She knows your woman's life . . .

And her devotion is to you now . . . from her spiritual heart to your human woman's heart . . .

Breathe . . . you are her, sitting on this chair, safe in your body . . . and she loves you.

She is devoted to you . . . to your longing for a deeply lived life . . .

Remember now and feel the closeness of the Beautiful One . . . Mary.

As you feel yourself back in the room, in your body, on your chair, in your life with all its stories, remember that you are loved from the heart of devotion and wisdom . . . the heart of Mary Magdalene.

Please feel free to share your meditation experiences or the images that may have come to you. The images that come to us in meditation deepen our connection to the story.

XX JOURNAL QUESTIONS

Mary Magdalene's status was purposefully reduced. Have you ever had that experience?

Why do you think this happened as Christianity developed?

What do you think our Christian church would have been like if Mary Magdalene hadn't been denigrated?

LESSON 4

Why We Need the Bride

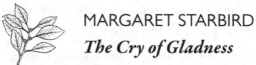

MARGARET STARBIRD
The Cry of Gladness

For two thousand years the Christian West has had a prevailing patriarchal model of reality, an exclusively male Trinity with a heavenly Father and Son seated on golden thrones in a celestial throne room. The esoteric adage "As above, so below" applies to this male-oriented reality and to the scenario that plays out on the ground in its image—the mirror image of what we worship. A preference for male children prevails across the planet, and the marketing phenomenon of violent video games for youth is universal. Adolescent males seem to enjoy things that go "bang!" in the night. Stripped of its feminine partner, the masculine principle becomes selfish, hedonistic, and violent. The "voice of the Bride" and the cries of the little ones can barely be heard above the din of roadside explosions.

Since time immemorial, the mystical experience of union with the Divine has been expressed in the vocabulary of marriage and sexual ecstasy. One of its most beautiful expressions is found in the Hebrew Bible's Song of Songs, where the bride and bridegroom extol one another's virtues in erotic language, celebrating their passion with mutual admiration. This is the language of lovers, the beloveds trysting in the garden. Rabbis characterized the Song as a metaphor for God's passionate and enduring love for Israel, his Bride.

We easily recognize the marriage covenant as a relationship of equality and mutuality, each partner striving to please and fulfill the desires of the other. The parent/child relationship is hierarchical, the child dependent on the parent, while the ideal marriage covenant is grounded in self-sacrifice of each partner on behalf of the other: a symbiosis that creates a greater good for both partners, bringing them joy and fulfillment in their relationship. It is this relationship that the Divine desires with each individual soul—one based on total trust and service to each other, with no holds barred. Our love for the Divine is only a shadow of God's love and faith in us. It is this relationship that is mirrored in the sacred union of the archetypal Bride and Bridegroom—the Divine Complements. This is the relationship of two equal entities, each formed in the image of their Creator, the very incarnations of the Divine as "Partners." This image of sacred union was to have been the heritage of every Christian but was sadly lost in the dawn of the Christian story when the Bride of Jesus was tragically discarded.

"There shall yet be heard the cry of gladness—the voice of the Bridegroom, the voice of the Bride" (Jeremiah 33:10b–11a).

REFLECTIONS and SHARING

We could restate the question "Why do we need the Bride?" as "Why are we created in God's image?" Unless we have an image of Jesus's Bride as a real woman whom he loves in the physical dimension, we can't really accept the idea that we women are created in God's image too.

All of life reflects a masculine-feminine energy partnership; it's the dance of creation. So the only image that makes sense is that of Sacred Complements, the sacred partnership of masculine and feminine. Together, magnetic and electric energies create and fuel the physical world; male and female energies create the human world. Their combination within ourselves creates our own developmental growth process. How could God not be the same combination? And if God is the same, how could God's story be different? How could there not be a sacred companionship story at Creation's center?

Mary Magdalene is named as the woman more faithful than the twelve male disciples and she is given "First Lady" status in the lists of women in the Gospel. We are told that she alone could both "hold" Jesus's agony and prepare his body in death. Jesus told the others to let her save her special healing herbal oil to prepare him at death. She was first to experience Jesus in life-after-death. How many "firsts" do we need to begin to understand Mary the Magdalene as First Lady, Bride of Christ?

Many were called Mary but only one was called "the Magdalene." It was the Magdalene who loved the physical body of Jesus in life and who was described in the Gospel of Mary as having ongoing communication with him after death. This tells us we can receive communication from God through the Sacred Feminine dimension inside ourselves. Mary Magdalene saw his death, saw his spirit body, and heard him talk from the other world. Goodness! We'd better reevaluate her place in Christianity, as she is so clearly a partner to Jesus's mission on Earth.

Together in sacred partnership they represent God as physical Divinity, Bride and Bridegroom.

Does anyone have thoughts to share on the idea of a flesh-and-blood woman as bride of Christ?

BELOVEDS IN THE GARDEN

Breathe deeply to begin . . .

Allow your own receptivity to bring your body to a calm feeling . . . breathe . . .

Watch how your calming breath is allowing you to feel down to the toes of your feet and your feet on the floor . . . calm and warm feelings . . .

Open to the loving feelings of the Divine all around you . . .

Breathe in so calmly again and feel yourself safe on your chair and safe in your body . . .

Go now to the garden we have been told about . . .

To the garden where the Lovers, the Sacred Complements who are Divinity to each other, meet and rejoice in appreciation of each other . . .

This is your own garden of your own design . . . your favorite flowers . . .

See and feel and smell the flowers . . . breathe in the smell of the earth and the water . . . a beautiful garden . . .

Breathe deeply again . . . take a minute to be with the details of your own making . . .

In this garden you are the Bride . . . you have on a bridal gown . . .

This is the garden where you will meet your Sacred Partner of this day . . .

Envision your dress . . . let yourself go in your imagination . . . picture the details of fabric you love and color you love . . . maybe ribbon or lace . . .

Breathe deeply again and feel your body relax with the beauty of this dress . . .

Breathe deeply with your heart's recognition of the majesty of your sacred role as Divine Feminine on earth . . .

Stay in quietness for a few minutes now as you see and feel who might be there to meet you . . .

When you are ready, feel yourself back in the room, on the chair, joyous within the circle.

What were your experiences during this meditation? Do you have any images or perceptions you'd like to share?

XX JOURNAL QUESTIONS

If you were raised with Bible stories, how did you picture Jesus?

How did you envision "the Church" as "the Bride"?

Can you describe your feeling reactions to our story of Mary Magdalene as the Bride?

LESSON 5

Why Not Gnosticism?

MARGARET STARBIRD
Consecrated Matter

The first-century Jewish philosopher Philo of Alexandria proclaimed, "Man symbolizes reason, woman perception through the senses." He was articulating a prevailing worldview of his time—that men operated from a rational, intellectual orientation, while women's orientation was experiential, based on the five senses. More generally, feminine wisdom is seen as intuitive and emotional, derived from personal encounter with reality. These masculine and feminine preferences are often called "left brained" (rational) and "right brained" (artistic). Working together, these two functions provide a balanced and integrated perception of reality in what we call the "sacred partnership" of masculine and feminine consciousness. This partnership is sometimes expressed as the union of Logos and Sophia, reason and intuition, divinity and matter. Ultimately the sacred partnership reflects the union of wave and particle, energy and matter, interwoven in an eternal symbiosis of the polarities. This is the "cosmic dance"—reality itself.

Many analogies and metaphors are used to express this intimate union or wholeness manifested as masculine and feminine energies. In one Gnostic text, Sophia is called the "Mirror of God's Divinity," since the created cosmos (matter) is seen to reflect the power and glory of the creative force, just as the sea reflects the sky and the moon the light of the sun. In the Book of Genesis, the sun, moon, stars, and planets are created by God, and God proclaims their goodness. Judaism celebrated the created universe, the earth, the delights of living, the joys of food, drink, sex, and the goodness of all creation.

But in the fourth century BCE, Sophia—feminine consciousness—was abandoned by the very philosophers who had once sought her wisdom. Instead of being the "lovers of Sophia" that the word *philosopher* implies, Plato and his colleagues became "lovers of Logos" (reason). Plato envisioned the divine spark of consciousness trapped or imprisoned in the physical body of each human being, longing to be set free to return to its spiritual home. The Jewish belief that humans were "vessels" molded by a Divine Potter and used in his service was lost to the Greeks. During the Greco-Roman era, a pessimistic Gnostic worldview evolved, which denigrated matter and extolled the spirit, while claiming that the earth, matter, and human flesh were the creation of a lesser god. The dualistic views of second- and third-century Gnostics denied the goodness of flesh, matter, and the earth, insisting on the abnegation of the flesh and the joys of being fully human. By the third century, the memory of the sacred marriage at the heart of the Christian story had been lost, and the voice and power of Mary Magdalene were stolen when she was declared a prostitute, identified with the "sinner from the town" in Luke's Gospel.

In the face of Roman persecution and an ascetic backlash against the hedonistic excesses of the Roman Empire, Paul and other fathers of Christianity were encouraged to extol virginity and celibacy, or remaining "pure" for union with the heavenly Bridegroom. A disdain for the physical realm and the body became entrenched in Christianity, totally at odds with the ministry of Jesus, who healed the sick, fed the hungry, and enjoyed sharing food and wine with his friends, encouraging them to follow his example: "Whatsoever you do unto the least of my brethren you do also unto me." Jesus came to lift the burdens of the law, to restore "life abundant"—not just on the spiritual plane, as the Gnostic doctrines suggested. With the loss of Mary Magdalene, the original holistic vision of the Christian message was distorted; the belief in the human person cherished as a consecrated container of the Divine was lost. In reclaiming her, we restore the image of the Divine as the Beloved Complements, Logos and Sophia.

REFLECTIONS and SHARING

At least the Church recognized Mary Magdalene as an "earthy" woman, a representation of a flesh-and-blood person with a heart full of devotion and love. There was no doubt that she was seen in the role of "pilgrim soul" in her search and longing for union with God.

Her story was always about the search and the experience and the wisdom gained in the body, with the body's feeling life. She stayed with her body's ability to love and to create new life within herself. She represents womankind's devotion and love for life and Earth.

In her story we know ourselves as sacred vessels of divine life. Through Jesus's physical love for Mary Magdalene as his Bride, we know he held body and Earth as sacred. The rejection of their Holy Union came from the disciples who questioned Jesus's love for Mary the Magdalene. And Peter built his Church upon this rejection. But there were others who did not choose the pathway of escape from body and life and love. Today we are rediscovering those followers of Jesus and Mary who refused to say "spirit is good, body is bad."

Perhaps we've come to the conclusion of the experiment with denial of the Bride and body, which has made it clear that to survive we must truly love our Earth-body and each other in community. We need more than union on the mystical plane; we need union on the physical plane to heal our world. Union is the love story of Jesus and Mary Magdalene.

Do we want to discuss the idea that rejection of Mary Magdalene as Bride grew into rejection of women and rejection of earthly life itself?

 ## OUR SACRED BODY

Sit quietly now and begin to feel the warmth again of your feet upon the floor and upon Mother Earth below . . .

Now breathe deeply in and out of your beautiful body . . .

Your breathing slowly and serenely tells you that you are safe . . .

If the spiritual importance of your body is denied, how can you feel safe?

Breathe slowly again . . .

When you feel safe, loved, and held as sacred in your body . . . you know your world as good.

Breathe again and let your compassion flow to your body and all it has been through . . .

Say to yourself, "I feel love right now in this moment for my whole body, knowing myself as 'the Magdalene' . . .

"Knowing how Jesus loved Mary Magdalene, let me feel love flowing to me as a woman" . . .

Breathe . . .

In your mind's eye see them together in their loving embrace . . .

　　Remain quiet for a few minutes as you see the loving embrace of Jesus and Mary and know this love to be yours as well . . .

　　Continue in silence for a few minutes . . .

　　When you are ready, feel yourself back in the room, on the chair, safe within the circle.

──────────

Did anyone have meditation experiences they would like to share?

XX　JOURNAL QUESTIONS

Gnosis means "spiritual insight," "intuitive knowing." Women have insights and intuitions all the time, and we know we don't have to deny the body to be spiritual. You may not call your insights "gnosis," but can you describe how they come to you?

Women's wisdom is wisdom gained from experience; it is more rooted in body experience. What wisdom have you learned from your body's life?

LESSON 6

Who Meets Jesus in the Garden?

MARGARET STARBIRD
The Garden as Metaphor

Since time before memory, the garden has been an image of blessing and delight, found in the first book of the Hebrew Bible as the "Garden of Eden," an image of primeval peace and harmony. The word *paradise* means "enclosed garden," so the image is associated with eternal bliss. The image reminds us of "original blessing"—the gifts of the Creator in all their variety and interconnectedness. Restoring the Garden is the eternal hope of modern humanity's attempts to clean up the environment and restore balance in ecology. We have awakened to the idea that poisoning the land, oceans, and air of planet Earth—our physical home—is toxic to the entire human family. In one amazing image of Sophia recently displayed in the chapel of the Theological Union in Washington, D.C., she is surrounded by infinite varieties of plants and animals. All of creation is her domain, in all its manifested glory, balance, and intricate interdependence.

The image of the enclosed garden is found in the erotic love poem the Song of Songs as a metaphor for the Bride: "You are a garden enclosed, my sister, my spouse; an enclosed garden, a fountain sealed." The fragrances of spices, ripe fruits, and beautiful flowers inundate the senses. In this ecstatic Song, the lovers celebrate their reunion in the garden, intoxicated by one another's charms and the burgeoning fecundity all around them—the garden of all delights!

One of my favorite stories is *The Secret Garden* by Frances Hodgson Burnett. The story echoes the prevailing theme of Western civilization: the lost Sacred Feminine and the wasteland that awaits healing. An orphan, Mary, comes to live with her uncle, who is a hunchbacked cripple, desolated by the death of his beloved wife. He has locked up the walled garden where she died and thrown away the key. He has also rejected his son Colin, who is sickly and miserable. After Mary comes to live in the manor, a raven, the oracular bird of Apollo, shows her the key to the abandoned garden. Mary works to set it in order, eventually letting her cousin Colin share the secret. In the process of reclaiming the lost garden, Colin is healed of his infirmities and eventually Colin's father is brought into the restored garden.

This story, amazingly intuitive on the part of the author, reflects the sorry state of Western civilization, which has so long denied the feminine her true partnership role and as a result has become a wasteland. Her patriarchs—like the wounded king of the Grail mythology—are crippled and desolated. "Mary" is shown the key, and eventually health and prosperity are restored.

The garden is an eloquent metaphor for Sophia—the Divine Feminine or Goddess sometimes expressed as "Mother Nature." She is the Lady of the Flora and Fauna depicted so beautifully in the Unicorn tapestries displayed at Cluny, where each panel represents one of the five senses and the final one depicts the Bride preparing for her nuptial night in the bridal tent. In the Gospels, Sophia is incarnate in Mary Magdalene, the archetypal Bride reunited with her beloved Bridegroom in the Garden—as in the ancient mythologies of the "sacred marriage."

 REFLECTIONS
and SHARING

Ancient symbolism of "the Garden" tells us it is the place most expressive of the goodness of life. It symbolizes Paradise and the archetype of Wholeness and God/Goddess. It is where lovers meet. Our experiences of love and birth and growth and death and the beauty of it all are well expressed as being "in the garden of life." A fountain is often pictured in the garden as a reminder that the flow of everlasting love is ours to taste. We look at a garden and we feel good; it's natural to think of love.

Perhaps it is the symbolic picture of Jesus and Mary Magdalene in a garden, united in sacred marriage, that is returning today through all the women who love Mary Magdalene. Many artists feel urged to paint or sculpt Jesus and Mary as a couple. We've always had pictures of Mary Magdalene as "Bride in Mourning" for her husband at the garden tomb, and then his return to her in the garden also. This scene may be the most profoundly mysterious scene in the Gospel stories. We hunger for it every Easter.

In the garden of life we know we must extend our love into death as well. Mary Magdalene goes to the garden and weeps for her lost Bridegroom. The garden holds love, birth, growth, and decaying death, all a part of the ancient spiritual pattern called "cyclic renewal." All life, physical and spiritual, renews itself within this pattern through the interaction of masculine and feminine energies, physical and spiritual. Jesus and Mary Magdalene expressed this pattern, representing Heaven and Earth, King and Queen, Bride and Bridegroom.

We now have the eyes to see that when Jesus told the others to leave Mary Magdalene and her jar of special ointment alone because she would be the one to anoint him for his burial, he was saying that she was his Queen, his Bride, his Beloved.

Do any of us have thoughts or ideas to share about seeing Jesus and the Magdalene as a divine couple in the Garden of Life?

IN THE GARDEN

Close your eyes and begin to feel the energy shift inside you as you slow your breathing down and pull your awareness to your own interior self . . .

Just breathe again now and you have slowed yourself down already . . .

It's in the slow rhythms that your deepest feelings are felt . . .

Let's recall this song we've all heard . . .

"He walks with me and he talks with me and he tells me I am his own."

Breathe within the feeling of being loved that is created with those words . . .

You are in the garden now . . . feel and see yourself surrounded by plants and harmless little animals, and the song of goodness is in the air . . .

You understand now that there is someone else in the Garden with Jesus and she has the same kind of love for you . . .

Breathe deeply and slowly now . . . and . . .

Hear the song in a new way . . .

"She walks with me and she talks with me and she tells me I am her own . . ."

You can now recognize that you have a loving Magdalene within you . . .

Breathe . . .

And she offers love and wisdom to you as we walk the garden of life together . . .

Breathe again so slowly and let yourself imagine this Mary . . .

For this is a divine woman who knows your human woman's heart . . .

As she walks with you in the garden . . .

Stay in silence now for a few minutes . . . and come back into the room when you are ready.

Were there images or perceptions in your meditation time that you'd like us to know about?

XX   JOURNAL
      QUESTIONS

What do you feel and experience inside yourself when you imagine
   Mary Magdalene and Jesus in a beautiful garden?

As you imagine this picture, do you have any feelings you might
   "get in trouble" for it?

What do you think is the source of the fear about Jesus being
   married?

LESSON 7

The Vessel of Life

MARGARET STARBIRD
The Sacred Container

No other saint in the Christian pantheon is so universally associated with a sacred vessel as our Mary Magdalene. She is honored as *myrrhophore*, "the bearer of ointment," a twofold title, since in the Gospel story she first anoints Jesus at the banquet at Bethany and returns to the tomb after his crucifixion to anoint him in preparation for burial.

We need to realize that the symbolic images associated with Mary Magdalene can be interpreted on several levels. On the historical level, she carries the ointment that proclaims the Messiah and King. But she is also—in her person—the Sacred Container. Mary Magdalene reminds us that each person is created a sacred container of the Holy Spirit of God indwelling, in constant communion with the Divine by virtue of each breath we draw. Each of us is "in the flesh" an incarnation of the Life Force. We are "earthen vessels," filled with the Spirit. Mary Magdalene, the Beloved and favorite of Jesus, is the perfect model for our own journey toward union with the Divine. She is the visual embodiment of the sacred container or earthen vessel.

One of her other titles, "Tower" or "Stronghold," provides us with yet another metaphor for the Sacred Container. A stronghold is surrounded by a sturdy wall to protect the residents who dwell within. This reminds me of Martin Luther's hymn, "A mighty fortress is our God, a bulwark never failing." Mary Magdalene's very title attributes such power and strength to her as guardian and protector of her people. In anointing Jesus, the Christ, she conferred on him the power and strength of the people vested in her as their queen. She was the royal embodiment of her nation, the sacred container of their national identity.

In Christian theology, this metaphor continues with the understanding that—as Bride of the Lord—Mary Magdalene represents the community or gathering, the *ekklesia*. As Carl Jung suggested in *Aion,* it is incongruous to envision Jesus trying to embrace a building. He needs to embrace a woman—his beloved counterpart and Bride of his longing. Together they provide us with an image of the Self, and whose image is of a royal or divine couple. We ourselves are sacred containers of this symbiosis of masculine and feminine energies—Beloved Complements.

REFLECTIONS and SHARING

Much of the symbolism of Mary Magdalene demonstrates the symbolism used by humans throughout history to portray God's feminine nature in each of us, which gestates, births, nurtures, surrounds, and protects what is dear to us.

Mary the Magdalene as the Bride was expected and prophesized. As "She Who Knows the All" and "Stronghold of the Flock," she guides us in realizing our ability to "see" with our intuitive and feeling natures, in a way that will protect us and those we love. The word *magdal* means "the strength of holding people together in safety," and it can be pictured as a fortress, a citadel, a bulwark. It also conjures the image of a central place, a center. Mary the Magdalene was thought of that way, as both center of life and protector of life.

In art we see her most frequently as "the woman with the alabaster jar." Her jar of healing oil or herbs identifies her as a symbol for healing the body, the sacred earthen vessel that she is and we are. Jesus asks her to use her sacred oil at his burial, surely knowing the symbolic significance of this role as divine partner and wife.

The jar, the bowl, and the chalice are all symbols of God the Mother. The jar in all the portraits of Mary Magdalene became the chalice in the Holy Grail stories; the search for it is the search for the feminine nature of God, needed to heal the wounded wasteland.

Let's not forget two other story symbols of Mary Magdalene, which also speak of our capacity to "hold sacred": the tomb of death and the garden of renewed life. Mary was there in both, showing the feminine spirit's earthy wisdom capacity both to be emotionally present with physical death and then to go on into life renewed and experience new beginnings. Mary can bear the pain of the tomb when the others run away and Mary can meet the Beloved again in the "good news" of the garden. Holding secure in love is the gift of the feminine spirit.

There's so much to talk about here. Does anyone have ideas to share about Mary as the Sacred Vessel itself?

SACRED VESSEL, EVER RENEWING

Breathe deeply as you begin your inner reflection . . . feel the warmth and security of your body on the chair and in the safety of this room . . .

Breathe in deeply, filling with the mystery of life around you . . .

You yourself are the chalice we speak of, the sacred vessel of life ever renewing . . . known as the alabaster jar . . .

Breathe in a great sense of relaxation to the depth of your toes . . .

Know yourself as the chalice of God's creation . . . breathe . . . there is a lovely warmth in this slow breathing . . .

It is your own ability to be the sacred container for life that you can trust in yourself . . .

Breathe in this feeling of self-trust . . .

Life energy is created in you . . . flows into you and flows out of you . . . breathe . . .

Her title itself . . . "the Magdalene" . . . also means "sacred vessel" . . .

Breathe again slowly as you feel yourself to be Divinity's sacred vessel of life . . .

Life itself is created in the womb vessel that you are . . . and this is the ultimate mystery itself . . . breathe . . .

You are the sacred chalice for all that you choose to bring forth . . .

Breathe in and relax within the strength of your receptive self . . .

Be in silence for a time and imagine what might be in creation within you now . . .

Come back into the room and open your eyes when you feel ready . . .

How was this meditation for you? Do you have any images or perceptions that want to be shared?

XX   JOURNAL QUESTIONS

Do you recall having curiosity about Mary Magdalene's alabaster jar when you saw pictures of her?

Her symbolism is also the color red, and she was often painted wearing red. What words come to mind when you think and feel red?

LESSON 8

Symbols from a Dark Time

MARGARET STARBIRD
Symbols of the Faith Forgotten

Steeped in the traditions of the Roman Catholic Church, its history, ritual, and art, I was thoroughly intrigued in 1975 when I read a book by Harold Bayley called *The Lost Language of Symbolism*. The book contained hundreds of emblems found in paper manufactured in western Europe during the period 1280–1600, the heyday of the Inquisition. Bayley's text attributed the watermarks to heretics hiding their secret symbols in the paper used to print their favorite works, including vernacular Bibles copied and later printed in French, German, and English, and certain beloved secular works including *The Romance of the Rose* and the *Song of Roland*. Prominent among the symbols found in the watermarks were the fleur-de-lis, emblem of the royal dynasties of France, and the "grail" or chalice, but the most numerous of all the symbols—nearly 1,100 of 13,000 cataloged emblems—was the unicorn.

In 1975 I was enchanted by these watermarks and interested in their provenance, the Languedoc of southern France, and their alleged connection with heretics, gnostics, and Templars. The Languedoc was the region whose towns were burned and culture destroyed during the Albigensian crusade (1209–1250), a period of brutal suppression by the Inquisition. Apparently the tenets of these suppressed "alternative" Christians had survived in medieval watermarks. They had called themselves the "Church of Amor" and claimed that they were a people of enlightenment, in contrast to the Church of Rome, which they saw as being based on indoctrination and intimidation.

Their watermarks were hidden fossils of a "faith forgotten"—a faith that survived "in spite of dungeon, fire, and sword." They were "Proto-Protestants"—opposing the absolute power and repressive hegemony of the Roman Catholic Church. Embedded in the pages of their Bibles and favorite books, the symbolic emblems attesting to the tenets of their faith could be detected only if the pages were held to the light. Since "enlightenment" was their motto and the essence of their faith, the watermarks themselves were supported by the "Light of the World"—Jesus himself. The unicorn was an acknowledged symbol for Jesus, the eternal Bridegroom. These "gnostic" heretics believed that each soul is under direct guidance of the Holy Spirit and that each life is a journey toward the "Light." For them, the "way" or "path" was illuminated by dream, vision, and synchronicity, those moments when one receives a revelation or message through a meaningful coincidence. These intuitive means of accessing truth and reality are "feminine" or "right-brain" activities, created in the unconscious—and often manifested in symbols.

For several years I incubated the symbols found in the medieval watermarks I had studied. It wasn't until 1985, when I read *Holy Blood, Holy Grail* (by Michael Baigent, Richard Leigh, and Henry Lincoln), that I realized that the heresy hidden in many of these marks was the "Grail" heresy, the belief that Jesus and Mary Magdalene were married and that the royal Davidic bloodline of Israel's kings had survived in exile in western Europe. The unicorn was preeminent among the heretical watermarks precisely because it depicted Jesus as the eternal Bridegroom and king of Israel cited in several Psalms in the Hebrew Bible: "You have raised up my horn like the horn of the unicorn. You have anointed my head with oil." Supporting this hypothesis are the magnificent medieval unicorn tapestries, discussed in my book *The Woman with the Alabaster Jar*. Further support for the "Grail" heresy is also found in the Tarot cards, which contain many symbols found among the watermarks and which I believe are a significant, though secret, catechism for the history of the alternative Church that believed in the sacred partnership of Jesus and Mary Magdalene. Throughout the Middle Ages, brave artists and artisans—painters, weavers, and poets—kept this story alive in an underground stream of esoteric lore right under the scrutiny of the brutal Inquisition.

REFLECTIONS and SHARING

Imagine if we lived in a time and place where the penalty for loving the Sacred Feminine as Mary Magdalene was death. We would surely find secret ways to say we loved her and that we knew Jesus loved her too.

Western civilization has an artistic tradition of doing that very thing: expressing a forbidden belief in the Sacred Marriage Church of Love. Before the medieval Inquisition period, Mary Magdalene as Bride and Beloved was honored by people who named chapels, gardens, fountains, springs, and vineyards for her. She represented the land herself, as today we might say "Mother Nature" or "Gaia." But a time came when it was dangerous to say you believed such things. The tide was turning ever more strongly against the Sacred Feminine and women. Witch burnings were soon to follow, killing at least forty thousand women.

The secret signs and symbols often used to declare belief in the sacred marriage of Jesus and the Magdalene were double XXs, the blade and the chalice glyph of an A and V together, the letter M in many forms, and towers or castles used to represent Mary's title as "Tower of the Flock." She was often painted head and shoulders taller than other figures, for she was thought of as "the Great Mary." You may want to read chapters 5 and 6 of Margaret's *The Woman with the Alabaster Jar* to discover more of these interesting and deeply felt symbols.

Why does this matter to us today? Because signs and symbols of our personal beliefs matter in the long run: symbols are one way we contribute to changing our world. Symbols are often secret signs of hope to others, supporting dearly held spiritual beliefs. Symbols are a language of God, spoken in dreams and artistic expressions of all kinds. We need to see reminders of what we believe in; they support our sense of spiritual self-esteem. Sacred symbols of Mary Magdalene, both ancient and modern, are coming into women's dreams everywhere. We are being called from our hearts and souls to express our love and longing for the return of the values of love and compassion.

The people who pressed heretical Church of Love symbolism into paper as watermarks are our spiritual ancestors; they left us a "Grail heritage." They were defeated by orthodoxy at that olden time but they live into another day through us.

What do we think about a time when it was dangerous to display your spiritual beliefs in a balanced Christianity, a Christianity of love between masculine and feminine?

 ## SYMBOLS OF GOD'S FEMININE FACE

Breathe an easy breath . . . for love and wisdom come easily to speak to you today . . .

Allow warmth and comfort to fill your shoes . . .

Breathe the feeling of safety within your body and your feet on the floor . . . and the floor upon the earth . . .

Emanations of loving energy are yours to have from the earth below you . . .

Breathe deeply again into the knowing that love and wisdom are yours as surely as the sun rising each day is yours . . .

Love and wisdom have their own language and their own pictures . . .

Breathe . . .

Their language and their pictures will speak to you from within your own heart . . .

Breathe again slowly and see the garden you've been to before in your holy imagination . . .

It is a familiar place of bountiful life . . .

There is something new here today, a sign or a symbol or a person for you to have as your very own . . .

Sit quiet for a few minutes to let yourself see and feel . . .

Come back into the room when you feel comfortable.

————

Does anyone feel moved to share their meditation experiences with us?

XX JOURNAL QUESTIONS

Do you watch your dreams for "signs"?

Are there other ways you feel you are given messages and signs by God, your soul, your inner wisdom?

What symbols have carried deep meaning for you in your life?

LESSON 9

The Special Kiss

MARGARET STARBIRD

Sharing Breath and Spirit

The Song of Songs, also known as the Song of Solomon, begins with this request: "Let him kiss me with the kisses of his mouth" (1:2). The Bride is longing for the kisses of her beloved Bridegroom in this most erotic poem that expresses a physical union that is, in fact, only a shadow of mystical ecstasy. The Song itself is a Jewish author's reworking of liturgical poetry celebrating the sacred union of Isis and Osiris, the god and goddess representing the eternal Life Force in the cosmology of ancient Egypt.

What is in a kiss? A kiss is intimate because it is a sharing of breath. In Hebrew, *ruach,* the word for "breath," also means "spirit." So, in sharing a kiss, two people are sharing their breath and their spirit. The early Christians were known to have greeted one another with a kiss, sharing the spirit of love and reconciliation. But in the Gospel of Philip, Jesus kisses Mary Magdalene often, and—although the lacuna in the parchment manuscript prevents us from knowing exactly where he kissed her—we know that the other apostles were jealous of their intimacy, which they saw expressed in this special way. Clearly Mary was his favorite, his beloved.

Can we envision Jesus and Mary as a couple, perhaps holding hands in the garden as they strolled there after an evening meal? Can we envision Jesus with his arm around her, his head bent a little to hear what she was saying to him? Can we sense the tender looks that passed between them, the delight they took in one another's company and in one another's embrace? This intimacy, this union, was at the very heart of the Christian experience, the model for the apostles and brothers of Jesus whom Paul describes as traveling with their "sister-wives" (1 Corinthians 9:5).

Mary Magdalene is a pattern for the individual soul in its passionate quest for union with the Divine: "As the deer pants for the water brooks, so my soul pants for You, O God" (Psalm 42:1). But her story is not just about her love and longing for Christ. It is also of his love and longing for her, a story of love shared and consummated. We thrill to the knowledge that our love for Jesus is only a shadow of his love for us. The story of Mary Magdalene confirms this mutuality.

 ## REFLECTIONS and SHARING

"The partner of the Savior is Mary Magdalene"; so says logion 55 in the Gospel of Philip. We've heard over and over that "Jesus kissed her often and that he kissed her on the mouth." Even though the original text is damaged at that word, the surrounding text implies a very special relationship shown by a kiss. This particular kiss, given for others to see, was an echo of the most popular religious story-poem of that time, the Song of Songs. This was a version of the love story of all eternity, the love story that is at the center of all creation. All the world religions have the story of a god and a goddess in love, a love from which life flows, creation happens, and the land and people are blessed.

When Jesus kissed Mary Magdalene in front of the disciples, he announced in a symbolic way that he was not a king ruling alone; he was not carrying on the philosophy of one-sided masculine rule that was the custom of the day. With the special kiss, as with so many of his intentional gestures, Jesus affirmed that he was in sacred partnership with the Divine Feminine, embodied in the person of Mary Magdalene. We know that the original Christian community was a community of couples and that the women were called "sister-wives." The special kiss between Jesus and Mary Magdalene was one of the symbolic gestures that revealed them as "Queen and King" of this group.

Knowledge of the kiss of the beloved, the kiss that changes everything, may have been buried in the desert with the Gnostic writings, but it is a universal theme that always lives within us. A story that illuminates the story of God's creation and its workings cannot be destroyed; it will always move through imagination and come out in creative works. Perhaps the kiss between Jesus and Mary the Magdalene reverberated through subsequent centuries in fables and fairy tales, outside the orthodox world. Out through the imaginations of ordinary people came the stories of a special kiss with the power to awaken. We wait for "the kiss" and then we know a new life story will begin.

Perhaps our modern wasteland can begin a healing new story if we let ourselves remember that Jesus "knew her well, for he loved her more than us" (Gospel of Mary 18:13–14) and that together Jesus and Mary Magdalene and their Sacred Union can bring new life to the world.

Does anyone have thoughts or feelings you'd like to share about "the special kiss" being so important?

THE KISS

Breathe . . . and breathe in slowly again . . .

Feel the safety of Earth beneath your feet . . . feel her capabilities for devotion and caring for physical life . . .

They are yours too, for your body is made of Earth as well as Spirit . . .

Earth and Spirit is also a marriage . . . a partnership . . .

Womankind has always symbolized Creation because we are Creation . . .

Feel the deep safety of your feet resting on the floor and the floor resting on the earth . . . breathing slowly into the rhythms of the earth . . .

Your body is secure and safe within the story of sacred union because as women we are honored in that story . . .

Breathe . . .

Let the warmth and the relaxation continue to allow you to feel deeply comfortable. Breathing . . . slowly . . .

A sense of safety is your birthright . . .

All life is created in cooperation and partnership . . .

In your body and in your life . . . in your soul and in your spirit . . .

Invite an image of the Sacred Masculine to be with you now . . .

Partner to you, your sacred partner . . .

It may be someone you know and it may be a figure of your inner world . . . a bridegroom of this moment in time . . .

Breathe deeply again as you go into a quiet moment . . .

In your holy imagination allow your beloved to come to you . . .

In picture or feeling . . .

Remain quiet for a time . . .
Open your eyes again when you feel ready . . .

We are all nourished by hearing others' meditation perceptions. Does anyone want to share theirs?

XX JOURNAL QUESTIONS

When you were a little girl, did you imagine the wedding kiss or the kiss from *Sleeping Beauty* or *Cinderella*?

What did you think would happen to you with a special relationship or kiss?

Have you had dreams of "a special kiss"? It can signal a change being made in you, a new part of yourself beginning to develop. Can you describe your dream?

The Weeping Magdalene

MARGARET STARBIRD
The One Who Cries

One of the identifying features of Mary Magdalene in iconography is a tear on her cheek or a handkerchief pressed to her eyes. Her tear is often visible in medieval paintings and statues, reflecting the fact that the only Mary who cries in the Gospels of the New Testament is the one called "the Magdalene." This trait is reflected in the term *maudlin* in English, which means "overly sentimental." But it is one of the age-old characteristics of the goddess who cries over the broken body of her lover in the ancient pagan mythologies. She is the compassionate one, sympathetic and empathetic, moved to tears over the plight of her friends and family.

In the Gospels, while the Virgin Mary "ponders her sorrows in her heart," Mary Magdalene cries. She cries at the tomb of her brother Lazarus (John 11), and Jesus is so moved by her tears that he raises Lazarus from the tomb. She cries over the feet of Jesus at the banquet in Bethany (John 12) and wipes her tears from his feet with her hair. Here Jesus is moved to protect her from the complaints of Judas about the wasted value of her fragrant ointment. She cries at the empty tomb of Jesus on Easter morning (John 20). First the two angels seated in the tomb ask her why she is crying and then, a few minutes later, Jesus, whom she mistakes for the gardener, asks her the same question, "Woman, why are you crying?" Mary's tears recall the prophetic passage addressed to the "Magdal-eder" by the prophet Micah almost seven hundred years before: "Why are you crying? Have you no king? Has your counselor/mentor perished, that you cry aloud like a woman in labor?" (Micah 4:8–9).

There is no mistaking this woman whose emotions are so heartfelt and whose devotion to Jesus is so passionate. She is clearly the Beloved, faithful to Jesus throughout his ministry in Palestine and even to his grave. It is she who is the model for contemplative souls seeking union with the Divine—one on one, heart to heart. She is the mirror of Christ's love for us; her love for him is only a shadow of his love for her! Can we imagine her tears of sorrow changing to tears of joy as she encounters her Beloved risen in the garden, reaching out to her, clasping her close, whispering her name, that name which in its very essence reflects her tears: Mary—"the bitter salt sea."

In connecting with the tears of Mary Magdalene, we reclaim our ability to live authentically, to express deeply felt compassion, to rejoice in our humanity and the gifts of our five senses, culminating in our mystical union with the Beloved. "Those who sowed in tears shall reap rejoicing, and they shall come home, bearing their sheaves" (Psalm 126:5–6).

REFLECTIONS and SHARING

Tears happen when we love. In our Christian story the many tears of Mary Magdalene were often misunderstood or criticized by those around her, except Jesus. Perhaps the others had lost awareness that one of the ways the Bride of the Messiah King would be recognized was by her tears.

We believe Jesus knew that he and Mary Magdalene were enacting the ancient pattern of Earth's spirituality, the pattern of cyclic renewal of life. In those ancient stories, the queen of the land falls in love with a hero and chooses him as king and lover to give her a child; then he dies. The queen's love for him ensures birth and blessings for her land and also causes her great sorrow when he dies. This is the pattern of life of our Earth and our bodies, with the cyclic renewal of seed, growth, harvest, death, and seed again . . . on and on in never-ending abundance. Love, birth, death: Jesus and Mary the Magdalene lived this pattern.

Tears are natural all along the way, for it is a story rich in feelings, one that is lived by each of us. If there weren't tears, only our head and intellect, and not our heart, would be with us. Mary Magdalene lived the way of the heart, the way of deep feeling.

Other people questioned Mary Magdalene's tears, but Jesus was moved by her tears, because he loved her. He protected her tearful reactions, telling others to let her be and to listen to her. In Mary Magdalene's weeping and the way it touched Jesus's heart, we see God's intention that we should include the heart in our life journey. In Jesus, we see the masculine spirit moved emotionally by the feminine spirit's capacity to feel life deeply and to love.

Mary Magdalene's weeping lets us know that we are loved for our ability to feel our lives deeply and be guided by our heart.

Does anyone have reactions to these new ways to understand Mary Magdalene's weeping and her way of the heart?

TEARS OF THE MAGDALENE

Take a few relaxing breaths . . . sharing these breaths is one way we know how deeply connected we are to each other . . .

Breathe again and feel your whole body relax . . .

Imagine that your feet are feeling so heavy and so warm . . . and that your feet love their connection to the earth . . . so warm and loving . . .

Mary the Magdalene . . . we've known her for two thousand years . . . we've watched her face in works of art . . . we've felt her feelings . . .

She has the feelings we have known in our own lives . . . her eyes tell us how deeply she feels . . .

Breathe . . .

Breathe and feel the warmth of your heart and your body . . .

She loves . . . sometimes it seems a love too much to bear . . .

Crying can bring relief . . . renewing can begin . . .

Breathe . . . give your weeping to Her, for she has the ability to hold all of the feelings of your heart . . .

She is open and allowing and receptive to your life and to your feelings . . .

Breathe again slowly . . . remain awhile in silence and with your own images as you invite the Magdalene to help you hold your life's tears . . .

Open your eyes again and come back into the room when you are ready.

This was a deeply felt meditation; does anyone have images they'd like to share?

$$XX \quad \begin{array}{l} \text{JOURNAL} \\ \text{QUESTIONS} \end{array}$$

Reflect on times in childhood when you revealed your tears to someone.

As an adult, how do you relate to your tears?

Do they need to be hidden?

Do you criticize yourself for crying?

Do your tears ever bring insights?

Descent to the Tomb

MARGARET STARBIRD
The Cave-Womb of the Earth

Universally, indigenous peoples have buried the deceased in the earth, returning them to the ground, thereby tacitly acknowledging the earth as "Source"—the "Mother" from whom we came and to whom our earthly remains return. From "dust we are." And throughout the world, caves have symbolized the womb of the Earth Mother. Since time beyond memory, caves have been the site of sacred ceremonies celebrating life and death.

One of the most amazing sacred sites on our planet is Newgrange in Ireland, build around five thousand years ago. It is a human-made hill, circular, fully lined with enormous standing stones placed side by side. The interior is a shaft with two compartments on each side and a central space at the far end. Amazingly, exactly at dawn on the winter solstice, the sun travels down the shaft and illuminates the interior space, the "holy of holies," the womb. This temple—older than Stonehenge!—was built to celebrate the sacred union of the sun and Earth, on the exact day of the "rebirth of the sun." It manifests the belief of its builders in the "eternal return" of the Life Force and the balance of masculine and feminine energies in the cosmos. The story is repeated in other structures and mythologies around the world.

According to the Gospel of John, Mary Magdalene approaches the garden where Jesus has been entombed before dawn on Easter morning. Of course she doesn't know it is Easter. It is the morning after the Sabbath. She couldn't come sooner, because of the strict observation of the Sabbath. So she comes at the first opportunity, carrying her alabaster jar of precious ointment with which to complete the burial anointing of the corpse of her Beloved. She is amazed to find the stone that sealed the sepulcher has been rolled away. Tears streaming down her cheeks, she gazes into the dark interior of the cave, into the womb of the earth, shocked to find that it is empty. She turns away in despair, only to hear, "Why are you crying?"

Life continues. In tears, Mary encounters the risen Christ, embodiment of resurrection and rebirth, the eternal return of the Life Force at the spring equinox. Their embrace echoes that of the Bride and Bridegroom from other ancient rituals—those of Tammuz and Ishtar, Aphrodite and Adonis, Isis and Osiris. Religions of those god and goddess couples celebrate fertility in rites of hieros gamos ubiquitous in the ancient Near East. The Gospel narrative, beginning with the anointing of the King and paralleling the ancient pagan rites of the sacrificed Bridegroom, culminates with the embrace of the Beloveds in the garden—at the site of the empty tomb.

 REFLECTIONS
and SHARING

Even though Mary Magdalene's role in our Christian story has been so minimized, we are still told each Easter that it was she who first saw the risen Christ. Only she had the courage to stay with the tomb, with the dead body of her Beloved. The men had scattered in fear and for self-protection. She, and only she, had been told by Jesus to prepare his body at death. He had publicly put her in charge of attending to his burial by saying that she should save her costly ointment for this last anointing. No one denies that this part of Mary Magdalene's story gives her very special authority in Christianity. It was another instance of Jesus making sure she was seen in the role of his wife. Who else would go to weep over a man's body and prepare it for death?

She had a wife's courage to view the body of her Beloved. There are so many important wisdom lessons in this story, for death and mourning are part of the ancient spiritual pattern of cycles of renewal. What is loved is lost, and found again in new form. It is a spiritual story of death and rebirth, told from time immemorial in many, many religions.

Mary loved Jesus with all her heart and she stayed with him through death, crying and lamenting as any woman would. Her heart stayed with the dreadful experience; she didn't run away from it. In staying with her heart's capacity to feel deeply, she was renewed in life. She saw the Light, she was reunited with her Beloved, and she could then carry the story of renewal to the world around her.

It's the wisdom of love that tells us to stay with our sorrows and our deep feelings, and out of that will come regeneration and new life. Descent into our own deep self, our own deep feeling, will bring rekindled awareness to us.

Mary Magdalene showed us the courage to stay with what we love, no matter what. She lived the story of love, death, and new life again.

Do any of us have experiences or thoughts we'd like to share about Mary Magdalene's capacity to "stay with" her heart's love?

DESCENT WITH THE MAGDALENE

Close your eyes and breathe especially deeply . . . and once more . . .

Breathe deeply into your feet resting so comfortably on the floor . . .

They are a warm and settled part of you right now . . .

Feel a heavy feeling . . . the warm and good heavy feeling of your body on the chair . . . Breathe deeply again . . .

Within the strength of the sacred energy that you are, it is safe to feel . . .

It is safe to feel what needs to be released . . .

For that is one meaning of the story of Mary's descent to the tomb . . .

She had to let him go . . .

Mary Magdalene's was a forced and tragic letting go of her Beloved . . .

Yours may be something as simple as letting go of a season and the earth turning to a new time . . .

Breathe . . .

Maybe yours is a letting go of a phase of life . . . maybe it's a person . . .

Breathe . . . something is changing and it needs to change . . .

Slowly let your breath go . . .

Your body knows what to do when a time of change is here . . .

Breathe . . . the Magdalene knew how to approach the darkness of the tomb . . .

She knew she must go into that dark place . . . her heart as burdened by suffering as a woman's can become . . .

You are safe to have these feelings because you are within the arms of God . . .

You know this by the steady and safe rhythm of your heart . . .

Your heart knows what to do . . . breathe deeply again and allow the feeling of safety to be with you . . .

Change will come and the courage of the Magdalene will be with you . . .

Breathe . . .

She endured the darkness and she saw the Light . . .

Sit in the quietness and feel what it is within your own life that wants to change . . .

When you are ready, open your eyes and come back into the room.

This meditation can bring deep feeling and new images; does anyone want to share theirs with the group?

XX JOURNAL QUESTIONS

What have been your experiences with death?

Have you ever had Magdalene's experience of "seeing the Light" after a dark time, as an insight or intuitional knowing?

Journey in a Boat with No Oars

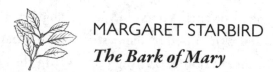

MARGARET STARBIRD
The Bark of Mary

Waves tossed the tiny skiff carrying political refugees from Palestine. Violent gusts battered their vessel as thunder roared and lightning crashed around them. The women huddled on the floor of the boat, a length of canvas drawn over them to shield them from sheets of rain pouring from the angry sky. At some point during that furious storm, the last oar broke and fell into the sea, leaving the tiny band of exiles at the mercy of the elements. Surely they felt abandoned. Unwilling to give up hope, Mary began to chant in her own Aramaic tongue ancient psalms that had sustained her people through centuries of exile and despair. The other women joined their voices to hers, in praise of the Creator whose will even the wind and waves obey. Joseph glanced at Lazarus and Maximus and then picked up the women's chant: "He will not suffer his righteous ones to be destroyed." Gradually their courage lifted, and they noticed that the storm began to abate and later to subside. Exhausted, they slept, rocked by the endless lift and ebb of waves and lulled by a gentle breeze.

Legends in Old French tell us of Joseph of Arimathea, the guardian of the "Grail," and of Lazarus and Martha, traveling together with their sister Mary and two other Marys, Mary Salome and Mary Jacobi, the mother of James. Several other friends are with them: Maximus and Sedonius, according to some of the legends. The French legends say that this tiny group of pilgrims landed at Ratis on the shores of Gaul in a rudderless boat with no oars in about 42 CE. This open vessel, defying all odds, was guided only by the breath of Spirit blowing it across the storm-tossed sea and casting it up onto the rock-strewn beaches of the Mediterranean shores of southern France. Ratis was known for its temple honoring the Great Mother Cybele, so it is perhaps fitting that it was here that the Christian refugees from persecution in Jerusalem found sanctuary. Their only salvation was their passionate trust in their God and his plan for their safety and well-being. Their journey, buffeted by wind and rain, tossed by tempestuous seas, is the model for our own voyage on the sea of life, trusting implicitly in the guidance of the Holy Spirit to bring us safely to our destination.

REFLECTIONS and SHARING

A boat is also a chalice, a grail, a place of "holding" life's journey. It's a symbol of the "womb to tomb" vessel of life of the Great Mother. After the Gospel tells us that Mary Magdalene was the woman who first saw the risen Christ and told the others, and after she met her Beloved again in the garden, she disappears from the official story. But that doesn't mean she's gone. We next find her in legend as a woman in a "fragile boat," crossing to France with two other Marys, her brother Lazarus, and a child later called "Princess Sarah," whom we understand as the daughter of Jesus and Mary Magdalene.

This is the story of Mary Magdalene traveling in a boat with no oars, guided by the hand of God to a new and unknown life in the south of France. Among the relics we have of this journey story is a drawing of a small boat on the wall of the Holy Sepulcher in Jerusalem with the words "We went." Another very early Christian relic is a prayer rug woven in about 150 CE that shows the Holy Family, with their halos and Jesus in the center, in a "boat with no oars." The story it commemorates in weaving is that the Holy Family of Jesus and Mary Magdalene went to France, perhaps fleeing in fear for their lives. In southern France Mary Magdalene's arrival is still celebrated in yearly pageants by the sea.

We can all find similarities in our own lives with this story of a dangerous passage to something mysterious and unknown to us. Perhaps we're facing a new time of life that seems difficult, or perhaps we're traveling in unknown waters inside ourselves, feeling betwixt and between ways of life. The theme of leaving something behind and the unknown ahead is a part of everyone's life. Mary Magdalene shows us the tremendous courage and faith it takes to "cross the great waters" and start anew. From her we learn that despite tragedy, disappointment, or just resistance to change . . . we can go on in faith that our vessel is sacred and a divine hand steers the boat.

We're in a new part of Mary Magdalene's story here, one you may not have heard about. Does anyone have thoughts or feelings about this?

SAFE JOURNEY

Close your eyes and breathe slowly and deeply as you move into your inner quietness . . .

Truth is made into story when it serves the needs of people's hearts and the circumstances of our lives . . .

Such is this story of persecution and suffering, journeying, and renewal in the feminine spirit . . .

Breathe deeply . . . there is a light within your head that grows brighter now as it reaches to join the bright light of your soul and spirit. This too is you. Breathe . . .

You're in your boat and you've weathered the stormy waters . . .

It's been really frightening . . . You've had no oars, no rudder . . . you've had to place yourself in receptivity to the forces of Goodness for your voyage . . .

You're not alone . . . you are with your loved ones . . . breathe . . .

You don't have to be a lone hero through life; you go with family . . .

Breathe slowly again . . . this is the way of the Divine Mother . . .

Breathe into the feeling of being with people you love . . . both here and in the other world . . . breathe . . .

You're safe now, the water calmed, and your weary boat comes up onto the shore of an island . . .

Breathe . . . see this place now with your inner eye, your holy imagination . . .

This is a sacred place of your own design . . . breathe . . .

It may be as simple as a grove of trees with an opening place for prayer . . . or as elaborate as a church for the Divine Mother . . .

Take a moment to see and feel the details around you . . .

You are safe here and you can lay down the burdens of your journey and give thanks for safe passage and for the help you've had along the way . . .

Breathe slowly and deeply . . . feel your thanks and gratitude for your body, for it is with your body that you've come through the struggle . . .

Sit in quietness for a few minutes . . .
When you are ready, open your eyes and come slowly back into the room.

Sharing perceptions and images from meditation is helpful to all of us. Does anyone have one to offer?

XX JOURNAL QUESTIONS

Can you draw on your own life experiences to talk about a time of unexpected endings?

Mary Magdalene didn't have to go alone; she was with her closest family. Do you think this tells us something about the nature of women's sacred journeys of change and transformation?

Who has been with you in your difficult times of change?

Bearer of the Sangraal

MARGARET STARBIRD
Sarah

Graphic medieval paintings of Joseph of Arimathea and occasionally of Mary Magdalene depict them holding a chalice catching blood from the wounds of Jesus on the cross, a literal interpretation of the blood of Christ contained in the Grail chalice. And it is Joseph who is later credited with bringing the "Grail" (*sangraal*) to the coast of France. However, if the sangraal (literally, "blood royal") of French legend actually refers to the vessel that once contained the royal bloodline of Jesus, then the Holy Grail of medieval myth is *not* an artifact, a cup or chalice. It is a woman. Woman as "vessel" is a very ancient symbol. A curious round pitcher from about 6000 BCE has eyes and breasts, attesting to the archetypal nature of the "feminine" as both nurturer and container of life.

The interpretation of the Grail as a woman—Mary Magdalene herself—suggests that she was the vessel of the blood royal. One does not carry the blood royal around in a jar. It flows in the veins of a child. Read in this way, the sangraal legends suggest that a child of Jesus traveled with family and close friends to the shores of France.

After reading *Holy Blood, Holy Grail* in 1985, I began to investigate the legends of Mary Magdalene in France to see if I could find evidence of a child. I was looking for some reference—maybe a symbolic one—to a son. I found nothing. But the idea kept calling to me.

One day I sat down at my computer and wrote a piece of fiction, telling the love story of Mary and Jesus. I was typing rather furiously, trying to record the thoughts that were flowing through me—their first meeting, their betrothal, the anointing at the banquet, the crucifixion, and Mary's escape under the protection of Joseph of Arimathea, culminating with the birth of her son in Egypt. Suddenly in the middle of Mary's difficult labor I broke down in tears. It struck me with incredible force that the reason the child had been lost, the reason that I couldn't find the child mentioned in the legends in France, was because Mary's child born in Egypt was not a son. How could I have been so blind? I had never even considered that the child of Mary and Jesus might have been a daughter! I wept. So unknown, unnamed, and unacknowledged was this child that she had been lost to consciousness, to history, even to imagination. I went back to the legends and combed them again to see if I could find any hint that a daughter had survived as a refugee.

A few months later, I had a rather amazing incidental encounter with a French woman from Saint-Tropez on the Mediterranean coast. She and I were seated together at a dinner party in an Irish pub in Nashville. Somehow our conversation turned to the legends and lore of her homeland and she told me about the legends of Les Saintes-Maries-de-la-Mer, and the statue of Saint Sarah kept in the crypt of the Basilica of Our Lady of the Sea, whose face is black as soot. Every year Black Sarah's statue is taken from the crypt in a ceremonial procession and escorted by gypsy men in full regalia riding snow-white horses through the streets of the town and out to the shore. The horses stamp in the surf as the people sing hymns honoring Saint Sarah and the other Christians who brought the Gospel from across the sea.

Following our conversation, I went back to the legends. Sure enough, there she was: Sarah, called "the Egyptian." Surprisingly, she was black. She was styled as a servant of Marie Jacobi and Marie Salome, who traditional lore insists were the aunts of Jesus. I went to my Concordance, which has a section about the meaning of Hebrew names, and I looked up "Sarah." The name of the only child on the boat means "Princess" in Hebrew.

Could this girl-child be the little lost princess of Western fairy tale and folklore, often lost at birth, sold or given away as a servant, or locked in a tower? A relevant scripture passage comes to mind: in the Book of Lamentations, the princes of the royal family of Israel, descended from the tribe of Judah, had faces that were once "white as milk," but now they are "black as soot." They are not recognized in the streets. They have been deposed, sent into foreign exile; their "blackness" is symbolic of their total obscurity in their new homeland. Could this scripture passage apply also to Sarah, who, like Cinderella, is a "sooty-faced" maid-servant, a "princess" in obscurity?

Sarah is the most speculative element in my story of Mary Magdalene. We do not have a birth certificate proving that she ever existed. At most, we have a body of legends that weren't written until the Inquisition was firmly installed, so we will probably never be told the correct story of the "little princess." But in dreams we are aware that symbols often manifest as puns or plays on words, sometimes as phrases with double meaning—like "Sarah, the Egyptian."

Legends attest to the obscurity of Mary Magdalene in France, where she is reported to have lived out the final years of her life as a hermit in the cave at Ste. Baume, north of Marseilles. Is it time to lift her veil, to restore her and her daughter Sarah, forgotten daughter of a long-lost "single mother"—the Princess of the Tower—to our full consciousness?

Torn from their homeland, deposed and humiliated, stripped of their power and possessions, this royal family was sent incognito into foreign exile, where they lived a hidden life. The statue of little Saint Sarah is the embodiment of medieval rumors of the surviving bloodline of the Holy Grail, the "little lost princess" of Western civilization, daughter of the "archetypal Bride."

"I am black, but beautiful" (Song of Songs 1:5).

REFLECTIONS and SHARING

Where there is a Divine Couple there will be a Divine Child. It's the natural story.

We've seen how Mary "called the Magdalene" represented the people, the land, and the Sacred Feminine to those who knew her as Bride of the Messiah. Today we might say "she represents Everywoman" and all aspects of a woman's life. We naturally look to "Everywoman" to see her relationship to motherhood. We ask, where are her children? Sacred Feminine spirit is the mothering instinct within us, whether it expresses itself as children of our body or children of our creativity. Where there is Sacred Union of feminine and masculine, something will be born.

We find the child of Mary Magdalene and Jesus in the many modern legends that come from visionary people as well as written stories. Yes, they had a child, it is often said. Some say a boy, but our story of crossing the sea to France says it was a girl, the dark Princess Sarah, as Margaret has explained.

To recede into darkness was the fate of Mary Magdalene and Sarah, in hiding after Jesus died; then they came to be known as the "Dark Bride" and the "Dark Princess" in early European legends and fairy tales. They were in hiding until a time came when they could safely "come out." Maybe now is that time. In the present day we have the research to support theories of a more natural and balanced Holy Family, and we have the inner eyes to look for the ancient patterns of womanhood that these theories reflect. Perhaps it is time to let the Blessed Mother be grandmother and to let ourselves honor Mary Magdalene and Sarah as mother and daughter.

The symbols are there in France in the "village of the Marys." Princess Sarah, the daughter, is "renewal itself," every year, as her statue is brought out from her church and she is redressed in a fine new gown. Growth and renewal is the domain of Everywoman.

We have many pieces of art throughout the centuries that show Mary pregnant or with garments symbolic of motherhood. And we also have the famous stained-glass window at Kilmore, Scotland, which shows a loving Jesus and a pregnant Mary Magdalene embracing as a married couple. We know the Bride within ourselves as the sacred partner of whomever or whatever we choose to devote ourselves. We need the daughter Sarah as well, to be that part of us that is born and grows through our ability to love and care.

There's much to talk about in the story of the Holy Family told in this way. Do you have thoughts about it that you'd like to share?

DAUGHTER OF MINE

Close your eyes . . . breathe now like you know how to do . . . slowly several times . . .

Feel yourself growing heavy and very comfortable in your chair, your feet soaking up the warmth of Mother Earth . . .

Breathe again deeply . . .

Say to yourself: "There is a part of me that is the daughter . . . the new . . .

"Pictured in dreams she represents a part of me just now growing . . .

"With safety and self-support I bring new parts of myself into the world . . .

"And like unto my own daughter, I will encourage and praise my growing and changing" . . .

Breathe . . . feel the warmth in your heart for her . . .

Breathe quietly . . .

There is a sacred love that wants this growth for us too and we call her Mary . . .

She brings us safely across the great water to a new land . . . always . . .

She is ready to teach us in new places, for Wisdom is also her name . . .

Breathe in the remembrance of Her . . .

Deeply comfortable and deeply quiet within, take a few minutes for your own private remembrance of Her . . .

Open your eyes when you feel ready, coming back into the room.

Were there perceptions or images that came during this meditation?

XX   JOURNAL QUESTIONS

Mary Magdalene's protector on the journey is said to have been Joseph of Arimathea. It was he who went on to plant the Christmas-blooming Holy Thorn near the site of the first Christian church in the Western hemisphere at Glastonbury, England. As protector of Mary Magdalene, what qualities would you imagine him to have?

What qualities would you give such a man today?

What is needed to protect the Sacred Feminine within yourself?

We Carry the Grail, Hopeful Cup of Life

MARGARET STARBIRD
The Holy Grail

What is the "Holy Grail"? Although there is no absolute definition of the "Grail," many medieval legends tell us that it is the cup or chalice that once contained the precious blood of Jesus. Intrepid knights, clad in shining armor and mounted on strong steeds, thundered through the forests of Europe seeking the lost Grail, performing daring deeds along the way. They were looking for an artifact, the cup from which Jesus drank at the Last Supper, the cup in which he instituted the Holy Eucharist. "This is the cup of my blood."

European legends posit a real artifact, a drinking cup, as the object of later searches because it was sadly, even tragically lost. One poignant refrain claims that the Grail was lost because its guardians were found to be unworthy. The wasteland ensues from its loss. In one legend, the "Fisher King," ruler of the stricken domain, is himself suffering from an incurable thigh wound that can only be healed when the Grail is found. How pathetic is his plight! Meanwhile, his realm falls into ruin; rain fails, plants shrivel, people starve. What is the true nature of this loss?

In the prelude to Chretien de Troyes' twelfth-century poem about the Count of the Grail, there is a story of a domain where nine lovely maidens guarded the sacred wells, each equipped with a golden cup in which they offered water to passersby. But the lustful king raped one of the maidens, and then, following his dissolute example, the other maidens of the realm were similarly defiled, and the kingdom became desolated. It seems that the Grail is very connected to the honoring of the feminine principle embodied in women. When women are defamed and defiled, the domain becomes a wasteland. This principle is reflected in societies all across the planet. The masculine principle, when it is not properly in partnership with its feminine counterpart, becomes hedonistic and violent. Who has not mourned the loss of the Grail—a powerful symbol of our connection to the Divine Feminine?

In Christianity, the lost Grail is embodied in Mary Magdalene, the "sacred vessel" who, as mother of Jesus's child, "once contained the blood of Christ." The Grail is not an artifact: the woman is herself the sacred chalice, tragically lost. Only when we embrace Her can we heal the wasteland.

Only when we embrace Her can we heal the wasteland.

 REFLECTIONS
and SHARING

When we each hold our inner feminine nature as sacred, in divine partnership with the sacred masculine, we will be carrying the Grail in our own lives. From this pattern of inherent Wholeness in Christianity we will be able to heal the wasteland and perhaps our Earth will come alive again.

As Margaret has explained, the Holy Grail vessel is a metaphor for the womb of Mary Magdalene carrying the royal bloodline child of Jesus. As vessel containing the blood of new life, Mary Magdalene becomes an image and a symbol of the Sacred Feminine half of God. She becomes the Christian story's female principle, its Sacred Complement in divine partnership. She becomes the "Goddess in the Gospels," as Margaret says. Renewal takes place through her.

As we have seen, there are other indications that Mary Magdalene was understood in her time as the embodiment of the Goddess: she was "assigned" the title of "the Magdalene" and given a sacred number code in writings about her, both of which underscored her special status in the eyes of her beholders. In the Middle Ages a legend developed describing her ascension body and soul accompanied by angels into heaven.

She was Christianity's Holy Grail vessel, a symbol for the eternal truth and ageless wisdom of the feminine God. In our time now, we know that only a purposeful relationship to the living energies of the Divine Feminine can heal the world, in sacred partnership to the Divine Masculine. The Grail legends call this "healing the wasteland" by finding and holding the hopeful cup of life.

Mary Magdalene, Bride and Beloved, we love and acknowledge you as the Holy Grail, Divine Feminine, vessel of change for a better world.

How do you feel about seeing Mary Magdalene as the Holy Grail?

 CUP OF
ABUNDANCE

Breathe in very slowly . . .

Feel the strong connection you've made with the energies of the earth . . .

As women we are the Holy Grail . . .

We have a womb, a vessel with the mysterious capacity to cre-ate life . . .

It is from us that the world learns to nurture . . .

Breathe deeply now . . . breathe down into your feet . . . they rest upon Mother Earth, whose nurturing capacity we depend on . . .

Breathe . . . feel Mother Earth's continual receptivity to us and her devotion to us . . . she continues to nurture us in abun-dance . . .

Her great and mysterious flow of physical well-being is inside of us as well . . .

The feminine energy of abundance is our own Holy Grail-self . . .

Breathe . . . feel your body resting so safely . . .

You are vessel for physical life . . . yes, sometimes it is a baby . . . and sometimes it is the mystery of creative energy . . .

Feel your own receptive energy to the new life in yourself . . .

You are capable of providing it with protection until the right time for its birth . . . the right time for others to know about it . . .

Breathe deeply again . . .

You are so capable of devotion to what you love . . . breathe . . . What is it right now that you are in love with? What is it right now that wants your creative energy and your nurture?

Remain quiet for a few minutes with the image of the Grail, and see what is calling to you . . .

When you're ready, open your eyes and come back into the room.

Does anyone want to share their images, perceptions, or feelings from this meditation?

XX JOURNAL QUESTIONS

Explore everything in your life that holds, receives, nurtures, welcomes. Think about this on all levels: physical objects, emotional patterns, and spiritual experiences.

Find a wonderful jar or pitcher or bowl in your house and put it on your own altar or in a special place. You can use it as a place to focus your prayerful sense of abundance and your hopes for renewal on all levels of your life.

PART TWO

Prayers and Poems to Complement the Lessons

INTRODUCTION

Divinity and Devotion in a Magdalene Circle

BY SUSAN KEHOE-JERGENS, M.A., M.F.T.

I grew up in a loving but dysfunctional adoptive home in the 1960s. I was given covert and sometimes overt messages that women were less important than men. As my parents claimed to be agnostic, I never had a religious or spiritual foundation. I was, however, fortunate to have love and guidance from powerful women in my neighborhood. These women took me in and served as role models, awakening me to my own sense of self-worth. I became pregnant at the tender age of fifteen. I moved out of my home and was sent to St. Ann's (a Catholic home for unwed teen mothers). After a difficult and confusing birth I then suffered the agony of giving my son up for adoption. As I had no guidance or support, this was the only option available to me. It was a painful, lonely, and scary time in my life. At the time I felt no kinship to the patriarchal model that was conveyed at St. Ann's.

What moved me as a child were the many hours I spent in the forest roaming freely. I can truly say that my mother/parental figure was the great Mother Earth. This outdoor play nurtured in me the capacity to see and feel the feminine as divine. For this I am truly grateful. In my twenties, after years of reparative psychotherapy, this natural aspect of the Divine Mother became a meaningful source of empowerment. My dream life became my way of self-discovery and information from the divine. I began to have dreams of Christ as a guide. I felt a deep kinship to women as I became older and realized the power of women's circles. I began to lead monthly "Goddess" moon ceremonies, drawing in women who were searching for inner guidance.

These experiences led me to the Magdalene. I voraciously read all I could about Mary Magdalene as a great teacher rather than as a disciple. She is our model of the Divine Bride taking her place at the side of Christ. This insight provided a role model of the wholeness of both my inner and outer masculine and feminine figures. As a Jungian psychotherapist I was able to integrate these stories as part of my own healing. At about this time I had a profound dream of myself in the seventeenth century. I was a scullery maid serving those around me when I discovered a watermark on the ceiling where the plaster was bulging and soon to be cracked open. I dug at it and found a box that held documents that proved my birthright was of the lineage of the Magdalene. The box also contained gold coins.

My interpretation of this dream is that all women are a part of the holy lineage to the divine Magdalene: we are all divine; it is our birthright. It is time for us to regain our places of power as beautiful and brilliant women, as life-bearers and as teachers, thus restoring balance to humanity. The movement of divine feminine restoration is happening now. Groups of women small and large have made changes: small inner changes as well as large world changes. We have brought insight, love, peace, and great knowledge to those around us. That is what has inspired me to share these poems and prayers with you, dear ones.

HOW TO USE THE PRAYERS
AND POEMS

As Joan mentioned, in our Magdalene circle in Los Angeles, we have found that sharing an opening prayer sets the tone and focus of our devotional time together. Then we often read a prayer or poem just before the time of spoken meditation to encourage a quiet and reflective, receptive state of mind. We also end each meeting with a closing prayer, which provides both closure and continuity until our next gathering.

The prayers and poems that follow include the prayers that we typically use to begin and close, followed by selections that match the content of the lessons. I have written some of the prayers myself and adapted the others from other sources. I hope you will find meaning and pleasure from the collection offered here. Of course, it will be your circle, so you should feel free to bring in your own selections, suited to your group's personal meaning.

Blessings to you,

Susan Kehoe-Jergens

The prayer we most often use to start our circle comes from Reverend Dr. Kendyl L. R. Gibbons.

> *Thou art the sun of my heart in the morning;*
> *Thou art the dawn of truth in my soul;*
> *Thou art the woven whole.*
> *Thine is the grace to be steadfast in danger;*
> *Thine is the peace that none can destroy;*
> *Thine is the face of the need-riven stranger;*
> *Thine are the wings of joy.*
> *Thou art the deep to the deep in me calling;*
> *Thou art a lamp where my feet shall tread;*

Thy way is steep, past the peril of falling, thou art my
    daily bread.
Thine be the praise of my spirit uplifted; thou art the
    sea to each flowing stream;
Thine be the days that are gathering and sifted;
Thou art the deathless dream.

Here is the prayer we use to end each circle.

With My Heart I Bless You

Not with my hands but with my heart I bless you:
May peace forever dwell within your breast
May truth's white light move with you and possess you
And may your thoughts and words wear her bright
    crest!
May time move down its endless path of beauty
Conscious of you and better for your being!

ADAPTED FROM A UNITARIAN
UNIVERSALIST CHURCH PRAYER
BY DONALD JEFFERY HAYES

It Was Foretold

We expect to hear about earthly love in the great and abiding spiritual poetry of civilizations past. We expect to be told that the Divine loves us and that divine love is reflected in our earthly love for each other.

It has been said that the Old Testament's Song of Songs gave people reason to expect that Jesus would have a bride. People looking forward to the Messiah were also looking forward to his Bride. The Song of Songs was likely an echo of even earlier sacred love liturgy, such as this hymn to the sacred marriage of Inanna and Dumuzi. Inanna was the goddess called "Queen of Heaven and Earth" in the early Mesopotamian religion, which endured for five thousand years. Dumuzi was her chosen bridegroom, the man she loves in this liturgy. We've given just a brief piece of this epic chant; more can be found on many Internet sites.

Inanna's Love Poem to Dumuzi

Bridegroom, dear to my heart, Goodly is your beauty, honeysweet,

Lion, dear to my heart, Goodly is your beauty, honeysweet.

You have captivated me, Let me stand tremblingly
  before you.
Bridegroom, I would be taken by you to the
  bedchamber,
You have captivated me, Let me stand tremblingly
  before you.
Lion, I would be taken by you to the bedchamber.
Bridegroom, let me caress you, My precious caress is
  more savory than honey,
In the bedchamber, honey-filled, Let me enjoy your
  goodly beauty,
Lion, let me caress you, My precious caress is more
  savory than honey.
Bridegroom, you have taken your pleasure of me,
Tell my mother, she will give you delicacies, My father,
  he will give you gifts.
Your spirit, I know where to cheer your spirit,
Bridegroom, sleep in our house until dawn,
Your heart, I know where to gladden your heart,
Lion, sleep in our house until dawn.
You, because you love me, Give me, pray, of your
  caresses,
My lord god, my lord protector.

From the Song of Songs
Let him kiss me with
the kisses of his
mouth:
for thy love is better
than wine.

I Thought She Was a Prostitute from Magdala

Self Re-Creation through the Magdalene

The messages were sent out; the condemnation that
    Mary Magdalene was a whore. Powerful women
    who do not serve the patriarch first often reap this
    score.

Her flowing hair of red, her wealth and wisdom, were
    used as excuses to cast her out. She was stripped of
    her power and we were all taught to doubt.

We were scorned and burned to the core; some lost
    their lives through this ungodly door.

We know now we are not unworthy, we tell each other
    our stories of pain, as tools of learning that bring
    us back to the place that all women reclaim.

*Every new day I witness the awesome power of my own
     soul and body healing itself, and in healing the
     oldest shame.*

*I have the knowing inside that the energies of feminine
     creation are fueling this miracle.*

*In every moment it is impregnating each inner cell
     with holiness as if saying to me YES, YES to you,
     YES to each of us, YES to this life, this is the path
     of the spiritual.*

*For this I pray to be always true in the cycles not only
     of my body but also of my soul's destiny.*

*I am forever learning, open to the wisdom available
     and courageous in waiting and welcoming the
     new manifestations to take hold with purity and
     forever reject the labels of impiety.*

Amen.

SUSAN KEHOE-JERGENS

PRAYERS AND POEMS
TO COMPLEMENT LESSON 3

Other Ways We Know She Is the Bride

Outwardly, I see plum blossoms full to bursting,
    overflowing from my trees.
I smell the sweet freshness of oleander and pittisporium
    and it intoxicates me.
I feel springtime and warmth like the Earth herself,
    body is woman, round and round.
I am busy with life like those blessed women before me,
    blessed women with me now,
And those blessed women who will come.
Inwardly, I want to plant the seeds that best match my
    self-journey now. I will prepare the soil by stating
    my intentions.
I will tend to them, bringing fresh water and pulling

96

away the weeds of resistance, fears, and old
patterns that threaten to smother the new growth.
I seek and find the inner holy place that elevates the
good vibration of humankind and connects me to
my guides for my soul's journey.
I have help, I am worthy, and I am loved.
In this way of self-reflection, love, and diligence, I will
always have infinite abundance.

SUSAN KEHOE-JERGENS

The following vows are from *The Holy Book of Mary Magdalene: The Path of the Grail Steward,* by Jennifer Reif, a book of prayers, ceremonies, discourses, and festivals for the celebration of the Sacred Union. The vows express the idea of surrender to the Beloved, both the personal beloved and the sacred union with God. The phrase "by the bond of Asherah and Adonai" refers to Goddess-God, who represent the progenitors of Mary Magdalene the Bride and Jesus the Bridegroom.

The Vows of Sacred Marriage

I give myself to you
In accordance with the Law of Love
And the Mysteries of the Sacred Spirit.
By the bond of Asherah and Adonai,
I am yours in harmony and in friendship,
I am yours in love and in passion,
O Beloved Husband (Beloved Wife)

JENNIFER REIF, THE HOLY BOOK OF MARY
MAGDALENE: THE PATH OF THE GRAIL STEWARD
(BLOOMINGTON, IN: iUNIVERSE, 2008)

Why We Need the Bride

Women's Special Place with God

The Mary Magdalene within speaks:

Yes I was in the low estate women were held in, despite my being a
woman of some substance. I enjoyed the house and the family traditions
of stature, but the inner story of the times was that women were not
seen. In myself I knew different and had some memory of the matri-
archal times of power and regard. But I also had the knowing that our
time was unbalanced. I knew we were engaging in an experiment to
manifest our creator-selves. I knew this in my inner self and yet there
was the world outside the door. Yes, it was frightening; you feel the
fear even now. It seemed the vicious ones ruled all the earth outside
my door. It's true that where I went I was called "whore." The feelings
about women in those times were that way: women were whores who

could only be saved by rules to make them acceptable to God.

But we women have always known we were more than acceptable to God because we bear the children. The act of creation itself takes place in us. Yes, the jealousy of those who want to have all the power over life is what creates the rules for women. And so it was at that time in the extreme just as it is now in your time. Again, the thought of that stops your mind. Your earthly mind is tortured with the remembrances of this fact and the experiences you have lived through. It stops you to feel it again.

Those times were violent and cold as well. I held my knowing inside. I lived my life outside my feelings and without my heart, just as women do today: doing the work to be done and waiting, biding time. I began to hear of the man called Jesus. Truthfully I knew of him. He was not so unknown: he already had a reputation for learning and knowing. He was a strange man, not one mothers would welcome as a suitor, even though he was scholarly. He was a strange man, going about his own learning, driven by his curiosity. He was not making friends with life; he was not making peace with his life as it was. He had a reputation. I knew of it. There was much feeling between him and his cousin John. They were both driven and their mothers were great-allowing energy systems for them.

"They were carrying forth wisdom of the earth."

FROM *THE MARY MAGDALENE WITHIN*
BY JOAN NORTON

A Navajo Prayer of Reverence for Women
Dine Wind Prayer
Oh, Great Spirit,
How lucky can one be to know such beauty?
One can search the world over and not find this much
loveliness.

Her heart is pure, and radiates love and warmth.
It has to be, for she reflects your beauty that I see
    around me.
Oh Navajo Wind, blow softly upon this desert rose,
Embrace her always with your warm gentle breezes.
Fill her heart with the pride and happiness,
From a proud and noble people that she does come.
Whisper soft reminders in her ear,
"Never forget . . .
Never forget . . ."
Oh Father sun and Mother earth,
Shine brightly down upon her path,
Allow her to see the beauty in herself as well as in
    others,
Protect her and keep her warm.
Hide her in your absence from the despairs of this life.
Allow her always to walk in beauty.
Oh, Woman who walks in beauty like the night,
I am a friend who is distant and silent.
I will care for you always.

BY WOLFEYES,
FROM THE NAVAJO PAGE OF
THE INDIANS.ORG WEBSITE

Why Not Gnosticism?

When the solar principle embodied in Jesus, the "Logos made flesh" (John 1:1), is brought into union with its feminine counterpart, "the Bride," the result is the Holy City that has no temple and needs no light, for God is the Temple and Jesus is the Lamp. Streams of water flow from the celestial throne, nurturing fruitful trees. The nuptials of the Lamp found in the final chapter of the Apocalypse produce fulfillment of the ancient promise: "the desert shall bloom."

FROM *MAGDALENE'S LOST LEGACY*
BY MARGARET STARBIRD

God and Goddess of All That Is,
Come together in sacred union within my body, my
heart, and my spirit

Heaven and Earth meet in me, together to make the
    desert bloom.

SUSAN KEHOE-JERGENS

Prayer of Thankfulness for My Body

*Beautiful body, you are the handiwork of my soul's
making and for this I say thank you and may we
always walk in beauty.*

SUSAN KEHOE-JERGENS

Who Meets Jesus in the Garden?

I sing to the Mother Gaia
I sing to the Father Sun
I sing to living in the Garden of Life
Where Mother and Father are One.

SUSAN KEHOE-JERGENS

Hindu Marriage Poem

You have become mine forever.
Yes, we have become partners.
I have become yours.
Hereafter, I cannot live without you.
Do not live without me.
Let us share the joys.
We are word and meaning, united.

You are thought and I am sound.
May the nights be honey-sweet for us.
May the mornings be honey-sweet for us.
May the plants be honey-sweet for us.
May the earth be honey-sweet for us.

The Vessel of Life

A Celtic Prayer to Each New Day

God Bless to me this day,
Never vouchsafed to me before.
It is to bless thine own presence, thou hast given
   me this time, O God.
Bless thou to me thine eye,
May mine eye bless all it sees.
I will bless my neighbor, may my neighbor
   bless me.
God, give me a clean heart, let me not from the
   sight of thine eye,
And bless to me my children, and my
   spouse,
And bless to me my means, and my cattle.

CARMINA GADELICA,
CELTIC CHRISTIAN SACRED TEXT

Blessing Prayer of Ever-Renewing Life

As it was,
As it is
As it shall be
Evermore
O thou Triune
Of Grace!
With the ebb
With the flow.

CARMINA GADELICA,
COLLECTED BY ALEXANDER CARMICHAEL
(EDINBURGH: FLORIS BOOKS, 1992)

PRAYERS AND POEMS
TO COMPLEMENT LESSON 8

Symbols from a Dark Time

To the Light we bow.
I ask and call forth my soul to speak to me in my dreams,
I love and honor the tender spoken messages,
    sometimes so quiet to my ear,
I will receive you into my life, thy love and wisdom divine,
Let Light and living heart's wisdom meet in me.

SUSAN KEHOE-JERGENS

Through a Desert Without a Path

O sweetness of my life
You led me through a desert without a path,
Over arid land,
To this green valley,
To praise your love.

GERTRUDE THE GREAT (ST. GERTRUDE), 1265–1301

PRAYERS AND POEMS
TO COMPLEMENT LESSON 9

The Special Kiss

I receive you wholly Christ. With you I share my whole self. I will teach you the ways of my body so that you will understand the rhythms of the earth. In my special kiss I pass to you all that is sacred on this earth and at this time. For I have visions of a new world, one where women are treated as the sacred holders of life that we are. Together we make a whole. In that union, our marriage will be complete. I will take what we learn and teach it to others . . . that is the destiny of our union.

SUSAN KEHOE-JERGENS

Loving Tenderness

Loving tenderness abounds for all
from the darkest
to the eminent one beyond the stars,
exquisitely loving all.
She bequeaths the kiss of peace
upon the ultimate King.

HILDEGARD OF BINGEN

The Weeping Magdalene

In myself I have the wisdom of her.
She has given me bravery
Whenever I need it.
When grief and tears come,
Like her I do not waiver at the sight of dissension, but
*   I feel and lift myself*
In the face of danger.
I have the vision of myself as whole and the ability to
*   access this wisdom at any time.*
Like in each new spring, with each new bud on the
*   trees.*
Hallelujah, I am whole and I have risen.
Amen and Blessed Be.

SUSAN KEHOE-JERGENS

Descent to the Tomb

Then Mary arose, embraced them all, and began to
    speak to her brothers:
"Do not remain in sorrow and doubt, for his grace will
    guide you and comfort you.
Instead, let us praise his greatness, for he has prepared
    us for this.
He is calling us to be fully human"
Thus Mary called all their hearts toward the good, and they
    began to discuss the meaning of the teacher's words.

FROM *THE GOSPEL OF*
MARY MAGDALENE (9:12–20)

Peter said to Mary:
"Sister, we know that the teacher loved you differently
    from other women.

Tell us what you remember,
of any of the words he told you that we have not yet
  heard."
Mary said unto them:
"I will now speak to you of that which has not been
  given to you to hear.
I had a vision of the teacher and I said to him 'Lord I
  see you now in this vision.'
And he answered:
'You are blessed, for the sight of me does not disturb
  you. There where is the Nous, lies the treasure.'"

FROM THE GOSPEL OF
MARY MAGDALENE (10:1–16)

Journey in a Boat with No Oars

Waves toss the boat,
Merciless waves
Slap its sides,
Splash the riders of the deep
With brine.
They cling to one another
In the dark,
Chant ancient litanies
To the Holy One
In their native tongue.

Yosef, watchful guardian,
Questions the guidance
That bade him sail.
With heavy heart

He shields the woman and her child
from slash of waves and wind.
They show no fear,
trusting in their God.
What courage, what strength
imbue this woman
whose faith has brought her
to this moment of utter darkness.

Gradually the storm subsides.
The winds abate,
the waves, tamed,
now rock the vessel gently
like a cradle.
Serene on the breast of the deep
they sleep,
watchful Yosef standing guard,
custodian of the Sangraal,
the Holy Grail.

Now his cloak is dry.
Crystals of salt form tiny stars
as the summer Sun
dries away the water's spray
that hours since
threatened to engulf them.
His eyes burn and sting
from sleep unslept
and from the bitter salt.
What does he see?
A faint shadow
There on the horizon?

A pain-induced vision?
Or land?

He awakens his friends,
Points north across the sea.
"Look—our God is with us.
We have found the promised shore!"
Maximus and Lazarus retrieve the oars
Abandoned in the storm.
They begin again to row.

White beaches glisten
beneath an azure sky.
Cypress, citrus, bright wildflowers
delight their eager eyes.
The men leap into the shallows
and drag their ark ashore.

A tiny smile now flickers on Yosef's sunburned
     face:
he remembers Noah on Mount Ararat.
"We have survived the terrors of the night.
My sacred charge is safe at last—
The Sangraal, holy vessel
of Jesse's root and Judah's vine,
to be planted now
beside a nurturing stream.
Surely the Shepherd of Israel
has found for us greener pastures."

He helps the queen alight.
Her sandals in her hand,

she wades through shallow water
to crystal sands.
Regal she stands,
Breeze stirring her hair.

Her child is safe
and free at last—
Martha and Lazarus, too.
Fled are terrors of tyranny
and the sea's caprice.
Peace and joy envelop them.

She gazes tenderly at the daughter
Born in desert exile.
"Out of Egypt I called my child."
Sarah.
God's choice was not a son
To carry arms in battle,
scion of David's house and Judah's tribe,
strong lion to crush Rome's brutal fist
and claim the royal throne.
No. God chose
this time a daughter.

"What they sowed in tears,
they shall reap rejoicing
and they shall come home,
bearing their sheaves" (Psalm 126:5–6).
"And you, O Magdal-eder,
Tower-Stronghold of daughter Sion,
Through you shall it come.
The former dominion shall be restored . . .

But for now you shall dwell in the fields . . .
and from there you shall be rescued" (Micah 4:8–10).
Shalom. Amen.

FROM *THE WOMAN WITH THE ALABASTER JAR*
BY MARGARET STARBIRD

Bearer of the Sangraal

These three little prayers were written by our Los Angeles Magdalene Circle member Ruth Thompson; they are from her *Woman's Common Book of Prayers*, a book in progress.

Birth, a Chant

I chant of the coming, of the coming of a soul.
Give thanks for the child, for the child God's love will
hold.
As it comes, and it grows, I welcome it to earth,
I rejoice and give thanks for its life, health, and birth.

Birth

I give my body over
To nurturing this life,
I give my warmth, my blood, my bones,

I give my peace, my patience,
My rest, my energy.
I ask God for thoughts of joy
To soothe and comfort me.

A Hymn of Faith

Put your head on the breast of God
and She will comfort you.
Let yourself be kissed by God
and peace will come to you,
Her strong arms will support you,
You will rest and be renewed.

Put your hand in the hand of God
and She will lead you on,
Live your life in the land of God,
Her love will feed you; come,
The earth is her dominion,
Her love creates the Sun.

Hers are the ears that listen
Hers are the eyes that see
You are made in her image,
Mother, not trinity.

We Carry the Grail, Hopeful Cup of Life

She Is Born

For a moment everything hushes.
Then the balmy breeze whispers . . . Sh . . . eeeee . . .
     Sh . . . eeeeeeeeee
The ocean continues Sheeeeeeee Isssssssss . . . She
     Isssssss. Born, Born, Born.
She is Our Queen, the chalice, the Magdalene.
We hear her name booming in the thunder,
 and the grateful Mother Earth will never be the same.

We hear the voices of the midwives,
they will mumble over height, weight, and wholeness.
She will be bundled in a warm soft cloth blanket and
     hugged into belonging.

119

Animals will gather around,
bringing the rich warm smell of life.

She will be taken to a sacred cave, dipped in holy
*   water, and held up naked to the starlit sky.*
She will be received . . . rejoiced . . .
Her name pronounced and her existence proclaimed.
She will be called the Mary Magdalene.
She will be given gifts of frankincense, gold, and
*   myrrh.*
She will be daughter, sister, cousin, niece, aunt, friend,
*   Holy Teacher, bringer of the Sacred Feminine, and*
*   . . . the blessed Wife of Christ.*

Mary will feel profound loss and profound joy as all
*   women do,*
* and the earth's balmy breeze will cool her body,*
soothe her, easing her pains, her wrenching pains.
We will hear the whooshing waves over her moaning and
*   yell for joy with the booming thunder. Until . . . She*
*   is born.*
The bloodline will continue . . .
Saaarrraaaahhhh . . . echoes from the mountains and
*   the earth will never be the same.*

ADAPTED BY SUSAN KEHOE-JERGENS FROM
"SHE IS BORN" BY VIRGINIA KROLL

Rites of Passage, A Prayer

The spiral
The circle
Darkness
Then light

> *Hunger*
> *Then fullness*
> *Blindness*
> *Then sight*
> *The cycle is holy*
> *The roundness of earth*
> *The mating of nature*
> *God's love, then the birth*
> *In this beginning*
> *Help us remember the end*
> *The holy two-ness*
> *Completion-amen*

RUTH THOMPSON

In addition to the prayers and devotionals for each lesson, Margaret has given us her inspired version of prayers for the rosary and the wonderful story of how it came about.

The Magdalene Rosary of Sacred Union

One night about fifteen years ago I fell asleep with my traditional five-decade rosary in my hand. I had been praying intensely to the Virgin Mary for one of my daughters who was suffering a health issue. During the night, my tossing and rolling caused my rosary to slip out of my hand and to twist and break, and when I woke up the next morning, I found that the rosary had rearranged itself into seven groups of seven beads (*heptades*), while one bead had fallen off entirely and was lying separate from the rest of the rosary on the bedsheet. Gradually it dawned on me that I was being shown a new rosary based on the number seven, a "perfect" number associated with the Holy Spirit and the Divine Feminine.

The rosary celebrating the Virgin Mary was revealed to St. Dominic, the thirteenth-century founder of the Dominican Order that ruthlessly suppressed the widespread medieval belief that Jesus and Mary Magdalene were lovers. For centuries it has been used as a tool for contemplation, putting the devotee of the Virgin Mary in touch with the "Feminine" unconscious through repetition of the Hail Mary (*Ave Maria*) while meditating on themes from her life and that of her Son Jesus. Devotees of the Blessed Mother and her rosary recount amazing stories of miracles worked on their behalf.

Now I was being shown a similar rosary celebrating the Sacred Union and mysteries associated with the life of Mary Magdalene, who is the Christian model for each human soul's journey into a relationship of intimacy with the Divine Beloved. By meditating on the "Mysteries of the Magdalene," the most important milestones in her life, a person can connect with a template of this eternal "never-ending story"—the spiritual journey of the individual soul. In his book *Aion,* Carl Jung states that the "Self" is often imaged as a "divine, royal, or distinguished Couple." This is the goal of integration of the opposite energies and the "wholeness" and holiness that comes about within the individual persona. The "Magdalene Mysteries" celebrate this journey and provide a tool for its realization in an individual life.

Since my Magdalene Rosary grew out of the traditional rosary, it has many similarities with its prototype. For two of the prayers, I am indebted to the work of Neil Douglas-Klotz (*Prayers of the Cosmos*) translating the Lord's Prayer back into Aramaic, with amazing layers of meaning found in each word.

The Magdalene Rosary looks like the traditional rosary honoring Mary, the Blessed Mother of Jesus, in every respect except that there are only 7 beads in each group of prayers in the "circle" (instead of 10) and there are seven groups of prayers (rather than 5)—a total of 49 prayers (7^2) rather than 50.

MARGARET STARBIRD

You can create your own Magdalene Rosary, as Margaret has done, with knotted string or beads on this pattern of sevens, or you can order one from www.RubyLane.com/shops/sallynortonjewelrydesign. The rosary comes with the Magdalene Mysteries prayers listed below.

During the recital of the heptades of the "Magdalene Rosary" one will want to contemplate the milestones associated with her life. The first series of "mysteries" contains seven events from the Christian Gospels, while the second series is based on legend and tradition of her life in exile.

There are two sequences of Magdalene Mysteries. The first seven mysteries are the Gospel Mysteries of the Magdalene, while the second sequence is dedicated to the Legendary Mysteries of the Magdalene.

THE MAGDALENE MYSTERIES

I. *Mary Magdalene: Bride and Beloved*

1. Mary meets Jesus and is healed of seven demons
2. Mary's tears move Jesus to raise her brother Lazarus
3. Mary anoints Jesus at the banquet at Bethany
4. Mary follows the Way of the Cross
5. Mary stands with the Virgin Mother at the foot of the Cross
6. Mary meets Jesus at the tomb on Easter morning
7. Mary carries the Good News of the Resurrection to the Apostles

II. *Mary Magdalene: Bride in Exile*

1. Mary travels with Joseph of Arimathea to safety in Egypt
2. Mary gives birth to her daughter Sarah
3. Mary and her family escape by sea from Palestine
4. Mary's boat with no oars is swept ashore in Gaul
5. Mary preaches the Good News in Marseilles
6. Mary lives out her life in prayer in the cave of Ste. Baume
7. At her death, Mary is assumed body and soul into heaven

Here are the prayers said on the beads of the Magdalene Rosary of
Sacred Union:

1. Prayer to the Source of Life

O Mystery of Life, Birther of all that is,
Hallowed be Thy Name.
Thy Kingdom come, Thy will be done
On earth as it is in heaven.
Give us this day our daily bread
And forgive us our debts
As we forgive our debtors,
And lead us not into temptation
But deliver us from evil. Amen.

2. Magdalene Prayer (repeated on each of seven beads)

Dear Mary Magdalene, love incarnate,
Sacred Vessel, Holy Grail,
Chosen were you from all women,
And blessed is your union with Jesus.
Dearest Bride and Beloved of Christ,
Show us the Way of the heart.

3. Glory to the Source, the Force, and the Presence

Glory be to the Source, and to the Force,
And to the loving Presence.
As it was in the Beginning, is now and forever
    shall be,
World without end. Amen.

$\mathcal{R}$esources

INTERNET DISCUSSION GROUPS

Online discussion forums are a wonderful resource for keeping in touch with others who seek more understanding of Mary Magdalene, or who just want to listen in on interesting discussions. We have a few favorites, in which both authors of this book participate; these groups can all be found at www.yahoogroups.com.

The Magdalene-list is moderated by Loretta Kemsley, who brings wisdom, intelligence, and a good ability to referee when necessary to the discussions about Mary Magdalene and early Christianity. Eight hundred people participate in "celebrating Mary Magdalene" on this forum and the topics range from Gospel story details regarding Magdalene to alchemy, symbolism in medieval religious art, reader reviews of new Magdalene books, and notices of current conferences about the Sacred Feminine. Loretta also publishes a wonderful online journal called *Celebrating Creative Women* at www.Moondance.org.

Goddess Christians is moderated by Katia Romanoff of the Northern Way Esoteric Mystery School. She has well over a thousand members and describes her discussion forum as "balancing Goddess and God. [If you] revere Mother Mary, Sophia, and Mary Magdalene as Christian Goddesses . . . or revere Mother Earth, Shekinah, Isis, Freya, Asherah, Diana, Kwan Yin, etc., but still appreciate some of the two-thousand-year-old traditions of Christianity, you are needed."

The Path of the Grail Steward is a discussion group moderated by Jennifer Reif, author of *The Holy Book of Mary Magdalene: The Path of the Grail Steward*. Jennifer has members from across the globe who are interested in talking about Jesus, early Christianity, the Mother-Father God, and Sacred Union.

SPIRITUAL TRAINING AND SACRED FEMININE INFORMATION WEBSITES

So much of my learning takes place on the Internet now, so I've listed a few resources here. These sites change frequently and interactivity is "the order of the day." I hope you will join one of the flourishing online discussion groups or blogs I've suggested; they are so rich with individuality and *your* voice is needed among the many.

www.MargaretStarbird.net is Margaret Starbird's site, where you can read more of Margaret's theological essays and see the other books she has written and also her current speaking schedule, as well as additional educational resources about Mary Magdalene and the Sacred Union.

www.MaryMagdaleneWithin.com is my website, where you can read a portion of *The Mary Magdalene Within* and link to my blog for interactive discussion about "all things Magdalene."

www.NorthernWay.org. In addition to moderating the discussion forum Goddess Christians, Katia Romanoff has founded the Northern Way Esoteric Mystery School, which offers ordained ministry degrees online. You can see sample lessons about "Restoring the Bride" on her website, and much, much more.

www.KarenTate.com. Karen creates spiritually oriented travel journeys that provide education about the Goddess cultures and gives visual presentations about the Goddess. Karen also conducts "Sacred Sunday" services and hosts a weekly radio show called *Sacred Voices of the Feminine.* She is the author of *Sacred Places of Goddess: 108 Destinations* (San Francisco: CCC Publishing, 2006) and *Walking An Ancient Path: Rebirthing Goddess on Planet Earth* (Winchester, England: O Book Publishers, 2008).

BOOKS TO PROVIDE ILLUMINATION AND COMFORT ALONG YOUR WAY

By Margaret Starbird

The Woman with the Alabaster Jar. Rochester, Vt.: Bear & Co., 1993.

The Goddess in the Gospels. Rochester, Vt.: Bear & Co., 1998.

The Tarot Trumps and the Holy Grail: Great Secrets of the Middle Ages. Boulder, Colo.: Woven Word Press, 2000.

The Feminine Face of Christianity. Hampshire, U.K.: Godsfield Press, 2003.

Magdalene's Lost Legacy: Symbolic Numbers and the Sacred Union in Christianity. Rochester, Vt.: Bear & Co., 2003.

Mary Magdalene, Bride in Exile. Rochester, Vt.: Bear & Co., 2005.

By Jean-Yves LeLoup

Jean-Yves LeLoup is a Catholic mystic priest and his writings give the very deepest inner meaning of the sacred union pattern at the heart of Christianity.

The Gospel of Mary Magdalene. Rochester, Vt.: Inner Traditions, 2002.

The Sacred Embrace of Jesus and Mary. Rochester, Vt.: Inner Traditions, 2005.

Margaret Starbird's back cover review says this about *Sacred Embrace*: "In this remarkable book, we are invited to encounter the real Jesus, who became incarnate in order to embrace and consecrate flesh, offering 'life abundant' through a spiritual path of integration. Springing from Jewish tradition, this Jesus celebrates marriage and sexual union as a theophany manifesting the presence of the divine."

By Jean Shinoda Bolen

Jean Shinoda Bolen has written many books about the Divine Feminine. These two are particularly important to our Magdalene subject matter:

The Millionth Circle: How to Change Ourselves and the World. San Francisco: Conari Press, 1999.

This book is about the revolutionary act of starting a women's "circle with a spiritual center" to help heal our world.

Urgent Message from Mother: Gather the Women, Save the World. San Francisco: Conari Press, 2005.

Restoring the stories of Mary Magdalene is a part of the restoration of women's wisdom stories to the world. Terry Williams's back cover review says this: "How much we need the stories of women to restore empathy to the world."

Other Recommended Authors and Books

Invoking Mary Magdalene by Siobhan Houston (Boulder, Colo.: Sounds True, Inc., 2006) is a lovely book that offers new litanies and rituals for including the feminine dimension in your personal spiritual practices. Her guided meditations will take you to places Mary Magdalene lived in France, and she discussess many ways to continue on a Magdalene path of devotion.

Crooked Soley: A Crop Circle Revelation by John Michell and Allan
   Brown (England: Roundhill Press, 2005) is about a modern-day
   revelation on Earth of the Divine Feminine through the language
   of the universal science associated with the Holy Grail. "From time
   to time it is revealed again, and when that happens, culture and the
   human spirit are renewed and life on earth is restored to its natural
   state as a reflection of paradise."

*God's Messengers for Today's Women: Hearing God's Call Through
   the Bible Mothers* by Tina Carey (Denver, Colo.: Outskirts Press,
   2007) is a wonderful workbook that connects Celtic goddesses with
   Old and New Testament women. Tina bridges an important gap
   between the older religions and Christianity, showing that we all
   flow from the same source.

Growing Up Without the Goddess by Sandra Pope-Rollins (New York:
   Booksurge, 2008) is a "spiritual memoir" that chronicles a journey to discover and dissolve punishing patterns caused by secret
   abuse. The presence of Mary Magdalene leads the author to dis-
   quieting truths about what happens when a girl "grows up without
   the Goddess" and then guides her personal journey of recovery. See
   www.GrowingUpWithoutTheGoddess.com.

The Holy Book of Mary Magdalene: The Path of the Grail Steward by
   Jennifer Reif (Bloomington, Ind.: iUniverse, 2008) is a wonderful
   book for those who are interested in more prayers, ceremonies, discourses, and festivals for the celebration of the Sacred Union of
   Jesus and Mary Magdalene. The author also tells about her own
   personal journey from deep study of the Goddess religions to her
   personal epiphany about Jesus.

ART AND ICONS

So many women I've met at gatherings and within our Magdalene
Circle tell me that their creativity centers strongly on Mary Magdalene.

She is speaking to so many at this time, in many beautiful images. Here are just a few resources to spark your own creativity.

Alexis Hartman has illustrated this book and also drawn posters of Mary Magdalene for several public celebrations. See her work at www.greenbluegreen.com.

Sara Taft is an accomplished artist and member of the Los Angeles Magdalene Circle, whose work is with "the deep feminine." She has created many meaningful and beautiful images of the Magdalene at important times in her life's story: www.sarataft.com.

Mary Ann Sinclair makes wonderful silver necklaces from images of ancient papercraft watermarks, symbols of the medieval Church of Love, which we have talked about in this book. She calls them "lights from a dark age." You may want one for your altar. See her website at www.myrians.com.

Sophia Christine's website, www.sofiachristine.com, shows beautiful painted icons of Mary Magdalene and Jesus together as a family, as well as each one individually. So beautiful!

Nicola Sedgwick has made an exact, gorgeously drawn copy of the Scottish stained-glass window at the Kilmore Church, which depicts Jesus and a pregnant Mary Magdalene. You can see the window many places, including Margaret's website. We have this beautiful image at each of our Magdalene Circle meetings. Nicola's Kilmore Window poster is available through Finbarr Ross at www.CelticMysteriesJournal.com. While the poster cannot be ordered online, you can contact the store's owner, Mairead Conlon, through the site and she will mail it to you anywhere in the world.

Inspired Sculptures has little statues that you may have already seen. They do several simply beautiful ones of Mary Magdalene as "Lady of the Labyrinth" and "Keeper of the Sangrael" and also one of Mary Magdalene and Jesus as the Divine Couple. They are a "World

Interfaith Project" and have sculptures of other deities as well. You can see them at www.inspiredsculptures.com.

Regina Barton, another member of our circle, curates art shows and represents artists. Many of her shows are centered on Mary Magdalene and the Sacred Feminine. The art shows included in the celebrations sponsored by our Magdalene Circle have evoked a wonderfully enthusiastic response. For ideas, resources, or consultation, contact Regina at (310) 281-6289.

A Happy Note to End On

Our Los Angeles Magdalene Circle has sponsored two public celebrations of the Sacred Feminine, focusing on Mary Magdalene as Bride and Beloved. We decided to celebrate the sacred marriage of Jesus and Mary with a wedding cake all done up in a traditional and beautiful way with white icing and roses. The effect was almost magical and brought moments of profound insight to many. There's no denying the Bride when you have a wedding cake! The celebration of Jesus and Mary Magdalene's sacred union on the physical level of life, represented in the abundant beauty of the wedding cake, reflects the deepest meaning of this book.

Maybe you will want one too; it's long overdue.